Children's Ministry
Recruiting Guide

With CD-Rom

Gospel Light

HOW TO MAKE CLEAN COPIES FROM THIS BOOK

You may make copies of portions of this book with a clean conscience if

- you (or someone in your organization) are the original purchaser;

- you are using the copies you make for a noncommercial purpose (such as teaching or promoting your ministry) within your church or organization;

- you follow the instructions provided in this book.

However, it is ILLEGAL for you to make copies if

- you are using the material to promote, advertise or sell a product or service other than for ministry fundraising;

- you are using the material in or on a product for sale; or

- you or your organization are not the original purchaser of this book.

By following these guidelines you help us keep our products affordable.

Thank you,

Gospel Light

NOTE

Editorial Staff

Founder, Dr. Henrietta Mears • **Publisher Emeritus,** William T. Greig • **Publisher, Children's Curriculum and Resources,** Lynnette Pennings, M.A. • **Senior Consulting Publisher,** Dr. Elmer L. Towns • **Managing Editor,** Sheryl Haystead • **Senior Consulting Editor,** Wesley Haystead, M.S.Ed. • **Senior Editor, Biblical and Theological Issues,** Bayard Taylor, M.Div. • **Editorial Team,** Debbie Barber, Mary Gross Davis, Karen McGraw • **Contributing Editors,** Mike and Debbie Broyles, Dan Burleson, Kathy Cawelti, Willamae Myers, Barbara Platt • **Senior Designer,** Lori Hamilton • **Art Director,** Lenndy McCullough • **Cover Design,** Christina Renee Sharp

How to Use This Guide

For an overview of the steps you can take to effectively recruit leaders and teachers for your early childhood and/or children's ministry,

1. **Read the Recruiting Guidelines** overview on page 6.

2. **Skim through the Reproducible Resources** section that begins on page 27 to get an idea of the many kinds of awards, forms, logos, fliers and scripts available in this book and on the *Children's Ministry Recruiting Guide* CD-ROM. The 💿 designates that there are reproducible resources for this item in this book and in customizable form on the CD-ROM.

3. **Preview one or more of the short video segments** on the *Volunteer Recruiting Video* and thumb through the *Children's Ministry Recruiting Poster Pack* to get a quick look at the other recruiting resources available to you.

> *Looking for some motivation for the sometimes overwhelming task of recruiting? Read "Who Me? God's Call to Serve" on the next page.*

If you need some quick ideas for a recruiting or teacher appreciation theme,

1. **Go straight to the Reproducible Resources section** that begins on page 27. Look on this page to find an index to the kind of resource you need.

2. **Choose one of the ready-to-use posters** in the *Children's Ministry Recruiting Poster Pack* and/or one of the short video segments on the *Volunteer Recruiting Video*.

Who Me? God's Call to Serve

When God calls people to service, people always respond willingly, right?

Not if you're talking about people like Moses or Gideon or Jeremiah or Jonah. Time after time in Scripture, God's call to serve was answered by silence, excuses, arguments or just plain running away.

Does that sound at all familiar? Have you noticed that inviting people to serve in children's ministry sometimes feels uncomfortably like begging? Like asking people to do you a favor? Like appealing to feelings of guilt or obligation?

Why don't God's people willingly volunteer? Why does it often seem as though it takes more effort to get someone to help than it does to do the job yourself? Why do we need a big thick book full of ideas and strategies and worksheets and job descriptions when people should be lining up asking for the opportunity to love and teach children?

Why? It's good that you ask. And the answer is a simple one: Because human nature hasn't changed since the days when Moses and Gideon and Jeremiah and Jonah did their best to avoid God's call to serve Him. However, while that continuing problem is the bad news, the good news is that God's nature hasn't changed either. He continues to gently pursue His people, loving us, nudging us, calling us to serve.

Therefore, it is highly likely that there are people in your church that God wants to use in loving and teaching His children. These people may never have envisioned themselves sitting on the floor with a group of two-year-olds or guiding a learning activity for a group of fifth graders—just as Moses and Gideon and Jeremiah and Jonah had never thought of themselves leading God's people or telling God's message.

Our task in recruiting isn't to nag or manipulate people into service but, rather, to help people thoughtfully consider the very real possibility that God wants to use them to love and teach children. Just imagine, your recruiting efforts can discover, enlist and lead people whom God has already gifted (see Ephesians 4 and 1 Corinthians 12) to make a positive impact on the next generation!

Consider the benefits that result from effective, continuing efforts to engage people in children's ministry:

- The more people who get involved, the more opportunities there are for changing lives, building relationships and making a positive difference in your church and community.

- The more people who get involved, the less stress there is for those who are already serving. Their load is lightened, they feel supported, and they are likely to continue serving longer; satisfied teachers really do keep coming back for more!

- The more people who get involved, the more the rest of the church will be exposed to the value of ministry to children, increasing the potential pool of future workers.

> For we are God's workmanship, created in Christ Jesus to do good works, which God prepared in advance for us to do.
>
> Ephesians 2:10

So as you prepare and plan, contact and call, keep your eyes on the real goal of recruiting—finding and then supporting the people God has called to serve Him by fulfilling their God-given potential as teachers and leaders of children.

Contents

How to Use This Guide 3

Who Me? God's Call to Serve...4

Recruiting Guidelines...6

   Step 1: Plan Positive Publicity 7

   Step 2: Make Recruiting Everybody's Business 11

   Step 3: Find the Right Person for the Right Job....................................13

   Step 4: Make Training the First Step 21

   Step 5: Plan Time for Appreciation..23

Reproducible Resources 27

   Forms 29

   Job Descriptions...47

   Recruiting..57

      Skits and Scripts 58

      Themes...71

   Teacher Appreciation 91

      Awards...92

      Events 106

      Name Tags..112

      Skits and Video Script 113

      Themes..120

How to Use the CD-ROM 131

Throughout this book, the ☻ designates that there are reproducible resources for this item in this book and in customizable form on the CD-ROM.

Recruiting Guidelines

You can read more information about any of the guidelines by turning to the page number listed.

Step 1:
Plan Positive Publicity (p. 7)

Develop a churchwide campaign to let people know the good things happening in children's ministry.

Step 2:
Make Recruiting Everybody's Business (p. 11)

List potential volunteers, getting suggestions from people throughout the church as well as children's ministry staff. Ask everyone to pray for your efforts to help people find productive places to serve God.

Step 3:
Find the Right Person for the Right Job (p. 13)

Plan creative ways to contact potential teachers and leaders. Provide them with complete information, so they can find fulfilling places of ministry.

Step 4:
Make Training the First Step (p. 21)

Provide orientation and training so that each new volunteer is prepared for a good beginning.

Step 5:
Plan Time for Appreciation (p. 23)

Show your teachers and leaders that they are valued and appreciated.

I'm glad I'm a teacher because...

Step 1:
Plan Positive Publicity

Few people in any church, small or large, tend to have a good understanding of every area of the church's ministry. There are always people in the congregation who know little or nothing about the Sunday School, Vacation Bible School, weekday programs or other children's programs.

At first glance, this lack of knowledge may seem harmless. However, when members of the congregation are unfamiliar with children's ministry, the results are eventually damaging. A congregation unaware of children's ministry

▶ is not a fruitful source of potential teachers and leaders;

▶ is unlikely to provide the resources needed for quality programs;

▶ tends to select leaders and give priority to other programs with little or no awareness of children's needs;

▶ gradually drifts toward becoming an older congregation, losing the needed balance of young families.

> What our young people learn today determines what the church will know tomorrow.
> Henrietta Mears

Therefore, it is essential to set the foundation for your recruiting efforts by developing an ongoing plan to publicize both the need for and the positive benefits of your ministry. On a regular basis, enthusiastically present to the congregation information about the biblical command to teach children as well as the goals, benefits and opportunities for ministry with children. (Coordinate your efforts as needed with the leaders of other age-level programs.)

An essential part of any publicity plan is to emphasize the good things being accomplished. Avoid announcements that sound desperate (even if you are!). If you convey the idea that you just can't enlist enough teachers and helpers, you discourage people from wanting to get involved.

> About one out of five adults volunteer some of their free time to help a church in a typical week.
> Barna Research Group, Ventura, CA 93003.
> www.barna.org Research Archives: Ministry Involvement

People are willing to volunteer their time but selectively choose from those ministries that present exciting opportunities for service. Your publicity efforts need to help people know the answers to these questions:

▶ What is God accomplishing through this ministry? (No one wants to devote time when nothing good is happening.)

▶ How are the lives of children and their families being helped? (People respond positively to positive examples.)

▶ What are some benefits and rewards for those who become involved in your program? (People fear burnout—work that drains without replenishing.)

▶ What opportunities are open to those who want to serve as volunteers? (Give snapshots of tasks—brief examples—to help people visualize how they might serve.)

▶ Who else is involved? (People fear being left "holding the bag.")

Use a blank calendar form ✪ to schedule each month one or more ways in which you can communicate the good things happening in your Sunday School or other children's programs.

Idea Bank

Distribute inexpensive refrigerator magnets that display your program's slogan or logo ⊕. **Tip:** Encourage members of your congregation to use the magnets as prayer reminders for your ministry and the children it serves.

Create a Children's Ministry Photo Gallery on your church's website or a prominent bulletin board. Show photos featuring a specific age or class in action. (It's best to get parent's permission to display children's photographs.) **Tip:** Serving as a volunteer photographer is a great way to involve a parent or senior citizen in your program.

Choose a slogan ⊕ ("Nurture God's Children," "Serving Children with Joy" or "Teach a Child. Grow a Life," etc.) that briefly states your ministry's vision or mission. Display the slogan on newsletters, banners, bulletin boards, posters, buttons, personalized coffee cups, parent brochures, teacher handbooks, classroom signs, etc. The slogan can be expanded to several sentences which declare why your ministry needs to exist and flourish. Keep the sentences as brief as possible so that people can remember them, and focus on the most essential issues. **Tip:** If your church has developed a mission or vision statement, use it as a framework for your slogan and/or sentences, showing how your ministry is intended to help fulfill the mission or vision of your church.

Provide your bulletin or newsletter editor with a steady stream of short articles about your program. **Tip:** Include a Featured Teacher ⊕ column in the church newsletter.

Periodically display a variety of miniposters in various locations at your facility. Each miniposter can feature a slogan ⊕ about the value of children's ministry. **Tip:** Miniposters such as these are most effective when they are displayed for a limited amount of time and then removed.

Coordinate with your church music leader to occasionally teach the congregation a song one or more children's programs have been singing. Arrange for the children to sing the song through once and then help lead the congregation in singing along. **Tip:** If possible, have an adult leader explain what the children have been studying and how this particular song relates to their Bible learning.

Invite members of the congregation (or adult classes or small groups) to commit to serving as prayer partners for a specific teacher or leader during the coming quarter, semester or year. Suggest that prayer partners call teachers at least once a month to find out about specific prayer requests. **Tip:** Print ads for prayer partners in the church bulletin or newsletter and/or on the church website.

Display children's work from completed Bible learning activities (collages, montages, prayers, poems, etc.) on a wall, bulletin board or portable display panel. Locate the display where it will be seen by the maximum possible number of adults. If you have space for a permanent display, change the display at least once a month, assigning each class or program a specific month in which to display projects. **Tip:** Add a sign with a headline that catches people's interest and include information that identifies the class, teachers and students.

Place a video monitor and recorder in a well traveled area of the church. Play it before or after worship services, showing a children's class or program in action. On top of the monitor, place a sign identifying the class, the teachers and the focus of the lesson. **Tip:** Print an announcement in the church bulletin, encouraging people to view the video and explaining where the monitor is placed and what is being shown.

Regularly interview teachers and leaders during church services or adult Sunday School classes. Good questions to ask are "What's something you enjoy about teaching?" and "How have you benefited from being a teacher?" **Tip:** Invite your senior pastor to conduct the interview, thereby showing support for your children's ministry staff.

Serve coffee and donuts during a time when your program is not in session (right after the worship service ends, etc.) and invite the whole congregation to an open house in your facilities. (In a large church, give each person or family a ticket telling which room the recipient is to visit so that the crowd is somewhat evenly distributed.) **Tip:** Ask leaders and teachers to wear name tags ✪ and to display photos of their classes and recent Bible learning activities.

Identify the key leaders in your church whose support is most crucial for your children's ministry. These leaders may be the senior pastor, a church board member, the education committee, another staff member, etc. Plan ways to expose these leaders to your children's ministry. For example, you may ask a pastor or other leader to present awards  to teachers or to children's classes. It is also helpful to plan a once-a-year Meet the Pastor Day on which the pastor visits children's classes or departments to informally observe and interact with children and/or share a snack. **Tip:** Firsthand visits often have far more impact than any presentation you can make, so continually look for ways to bring church leaders into the classroom.

Arrange for a church committee or board to tour several children's classrooms as part of its meeting. **Tip:** Select as your tour guide an enthusiastic teacher who can explain how God's Word is being taught.

Include prayer requests related to your program in pastoral prayers, prayer lists and church newsletters, highlighting the entire church's commitment to the importance of the teaching ministry. **Tip:** Don't forget to share answers to prayer and how God is working in the lives of your teachers and leaders and through them in the lives of their students.

Encourage teachers to think of ways their classes can share some of their Bible learning activities outside of their classrooms—snacks the children make can be shared with youth or adult classes, sign language for Bible verses or songs can be presented during a worship service, skits can be presented live to other classes or videotaped for others to view, etc. **Tip:** If it seems appropriate when activities are shared, mention open positions for teachers or leaders in children's ministry.

Step 2: Make Recruiting Everybody's Business

Every children's director needs help in the recruiting process. In today's world, people can make frequent job changes and face constant demands on their time. As a result, new teachers and leaders will always be needed. If recruiting is the job of only a few people, they will soon become overworked and discouraged.

It would be chaotic if many people were working on their own to sign up new teachers! But key church leaders can support, encourage and, above all, pray that potential teachers will accept an invitation to ministry. Inform everyone on the church staff and other leadership positions of your recruiting needs. Ask them to pray regularly that needs will be met and, where appropriate, invite their help at specific points in the recruiting process.

It is often helpful to form a recruiting team of three to five people who oversee and put into practice the various steps of effective recruiting. When asking people to serve as recruiters, give them a brief overview of the job (use a written job description 🌐), what their responsibilities will be and why you think they can do the job successfully.

> If I could relive my life, I would devote my entire ministry to reaching children for God.
>
> D. L. Moody

At the first meeting of the recruiting team, give the members complete information about the program(s) or event(s) for which they will be recruiting. Distribute job descriptions for the open volunteer positions and lists of prospects. Plan who will contact each person, and agree on the next meeting date.

Recruiting Team Agenda

1. Get Acquainted

Ask each team member to tell a neighbor or the group a brief story about a time he or she was asked to serve in a church or community program. As time permits, participant describes a way the recruiting effort either was successful or could have been improved.

2. Guidelines for Recruiting

Present guidelines for making recruiting calls (by telephone or in person) and ask committee members to tell the benefit of following each guideline:

▸ **Guideline #1** Explain why the job is important and why the prospect is considered to have the potential to be effective at the task.

▸ **Guideline #2** Clearly describe the job and what is required to do the job effectively, and provide a written job description.

▸ **Guideline #3** Show the prospect the resources and training the church provides.

▸ **Guideline #4** Ask the prospect to pray and respond by a specific date. Offer the opportunity for the prospect to observe the ministry before responding.

Note: Complete information on these guidelines is found on page 15.

3. Recruiting Tasks

Give information regarding the number and kinds of volunteers needed, all applicable job descriptions, potential contacts, address and phone lists, etc. Agree on each person's tasks and set future meeting dates.

4. Prayer

Invite team members to pray for each other, potential volunteers and the recruiting process.

Idea Bank

List volunteer needs in a monthly staff memo or newsletter, e-mail or mini-posters displayed in a staff break room. **Tip:** Along with each volunteer need, include a brief praise report as well.

Ask your church's prayer ministry team (or an adult small fellowship group) to commit to a 30-day prayer covenant. Provide them with a list of children's programs and staff needs. **Tip:** At the beginning of the 30 days, briefly interview a teacher or child at a meeting of the prayer ministry team or fellowship group.

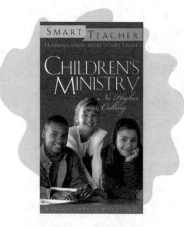

At the beginning of a staff meeting, show one of the segments from the *Children's Ministry* video (available in *Children's Ministry Recruiting Kit*), which highlights the benefits of children's ministry. **Tip:** Give the video to a potential volunteer to view at home.

Give a recruiting handbook 🌐 to those who will assist you in recruiting. The handbook can provide encouragement in the recruiting process; helpful hints for contacting prospective teachers and leaders; suggested guidelines for contact and follow-up of recruits; and a place to list contact names, phone numbers and responses. **Tip:** On the cover of the handbook, feature the slogan or logo 🌐 of your children's ministry program.

Make a list of the leaders of other church ministries (new members, collegians, seniors, singles, etc.). Provide each leader with a form 🌐 on which he or she may list names and contact information for potential volunteers. Avoid approaching participants in other ministries as a way to get people out of those groups and into your group. The goal is to help people keep involved in their fellowship/learning groups while finding the job of giving through service. **Tip:** Emphasize your desire to help people find places of ministry and growth that are best suited to their interests and gifts.

Get volunteer recommendations from current leaders and teachers. Give them a form 🌐 on which they can list names of people they know who have the characteristics needed for children's ministry. Emphasize that the list is not limited to people who have shown interest in children's ministries, but it should include those with qualities (faithful, friendly, caring, etc.) that God could use in this ministry. **Tip:** Also ask people to list the names of others in the church with whom they might like to form a teaching team for the upcoming semester or year.

Survey the people in your congregation, asking them to briefly list their talents and interests. Present the survey form 🌐 in adult classes or small groups, as part of a new member's class or as part of a worship service,

which emphasizes opportunities for ministry. Make a card file of prospects based on the information in the survey. Only solicit the number of surveys you can process. Make sure everyone receives a follow-up contact. **Tip:** You'll receive more of the surveys if you schedule a time in the class or worship service in which people complete them and turn them in before leaving rather than taking them home to fill out and bring back.

© 2003 Gospel Light. Permission to photocopy granted. *Children's Ministry Recruiting Guide*

Step 3: Find the Right Person for the Right Job

Much of what we desire of a person in children's ministry has to do with relationships. Most everything else—how to tell a Bible story, how to guide an art activity, and so on—can be taught. But relationships deal with more intangible things.

First, we want our leaders and teachers to be people whose relationships with God are foremost in their lives. That relationship is the foundation upon which all other parts of ministry are built. Let your own attitudes and actions reflect a desire to love and obey God in everyday life—whether it be in ministry to the children of your church or in serving the volunteers you recruit. Then look for others whose love for God is demonstrated in practical ways.

Second, children's ministry staff need to be people who are able to build relationships with the children they teach or lead and with the other members of their teaching team.

> *You teach a little bit by what you say. You teach most by what you are.*
> Henrietta Mears

To the busy children's ministry director, however, getting bodies to fill urgent recruiting needs can overwhelm the priorities we've established. It often seems that as soon as one position is filled, two more positions become vacant! The emphasis on recruiting then becomes one of filling vacancies rather than finding and nurturing individuals who have the characteristics needed for successful children's ministry.

To avoid this tendency toward the tyranny of the urgent in recruiting, allow ample time to identify, evaluate and contact possible volunteers. The benefits that result will be many:

▶ People will not feel they have to fill a vacancy because no one else is available.

▶ You can help potential volunteers find and use their spiritual gifts. (Some churches provide prospects with spiritual-gift inventories to complete as a guide to ministry.)

▶ A volunteer will have time to observe one or more ministries to find the most satisfying spot for service.

▶ You have the opportunity to match interests and skills with specific needs, rather than positions.

The first key to finding the right person for the right job, however, is to begin early. Start by identifying the positions that need to be filled (make sure to allow for appropriate ratios of teachers and children—one teacher for every four to six children in early childhood programs and one teacher for every six to eight children in children's programs) and listing the names of potential volunteers. For a new program or a special event, make this list *four to six months* ahead of time. For an ongoing program, update the list as needed.

Consider many sources for the names of potential volunteers (suggestions from adult teachers or adult class leaders, new members' classes, lists of previous staff and survey forms, etc.). After your list is compiled, involve other leaders in the church in evaluating or approving those to be contacted. Some potential recruits may need to be eliminated from consideration due to other commitments they made of which you may be unaware. Others may need to be removed from the list because they do not meet the guidelines set up by your church (membership in the church, attendance for at least six months, etc.). Follow your church's established procedures for screening and approving volunteers. (See "Screening Procedures" on p. 19 for complete information on developing procedures.)

Recruiting Time Line

Follow this time line for ongoing programs that begin in the fall of the year. Adapt the time line for other programs such as Vacation Bible School, weekday club programs or special events.

1. Begin in March to ask current staff if they are willing to return in the fall.

2. Estimate attendance in the fall, determine how many staff members will be needed and how many positions will need to be filled. Update the job descriptions for each position.

3. Collect names to create a prospect list. Prioritize the list.

4. Begin to contact prospects yourself or form a recruitment team who meets regularly for one to two months and assign prospects for the team to contact. (For more information on forming a recruitment team, see p. 11.)

The second key to finding the right person for the right job is to write or update a job description 🌐 for every position you need to fill. An effective job description clearly describes the job and what is required in order to do the job effectively. People want to know how much time, effort and ability the job will require. (See "Term of Service" on p. 20 for an evaluation of commitment terms.)

As a bonus, a job description can often help you recruit by describing what support and resources the volunteer will receive. Providing well-written job descriptions will give you a head start on your recruiting!

The third key is to personally contact a prospective volunteer. A personal letter or a flier 🌐 with a personalized note is a good first step, allowing the prospect to con-

sider the matter without the pressure of someone eagerly looking for an immediate response. Follow up the letter or flier with a phone call or a face-to-face meeting. A personal conversation lets the prospect know that you consider both him or her and the position important. A personal meeting also allows an unhurried period of time during which you can answer each other's questions and clarify information as needed. (Note: In order to show the value of children's ministry jobs and to avoid making it too easy to quickly decline, save e-mail contacts for appointment reminders, etc.)

Shortly before or at the same time that you are contacting prospects, you may also choose to write bulletin announcements, set up children's ministries displays, put up posters or put attention-getting inserts into your church newsletter. Keep in mind, however, that creative fliers, posters and displays can help communicate the need for teachers, but they rarely motivate potential leaders and teachers to make a commitment. Personal contact is essential because it communicates that the person is important and that a high value is placed on the ministry.

If you need to recruit a large number of people, it may not be possible to initially meet with every potential volunteer. An alternative is to schedule one or more meetings (offer dessert or a variety of coffees) to which prospects are invited. Encourage one or more experienced teachers to attend to share the benefits they have gained.

Whether your contact of the prospect is by phone or in person, follow these guidelines and complete a contact record form 💿.

1. Begin by explaining why the job is important and why you feel the prospect would be effective at the task, briefly describing the prospect's characteristics that qualify him or her for the task at hand.

2. Clearly present the position's basic responsibilities, giving (or mailing) the prospect a written job description 💿. In your conversation, focus on the program goals and the methods to be used. Tell the prospect the specific length of service expected. Make sure the prospect knows who his or her supervisor and coworkers will be and summarize other relevant information about the organizational structure of your church. It is helpful to let the prospect know that substitutes are available for weeks when he or she must be gone because of illness, vacation or other emergency.

3. Show or describe the resources the church provides for teaching, materials, visual aids, supplies, etc. (If your curriculum provides a sample kit for various age levels, have it available for the prospect to examine.) Explain what the church offers in terms of training and support. Provide the opportunity for the prospect to observe a current session where someone is doing the same (or similar) job to the one you are asking the prospect to consider. Give the prospect an observation form 💿 to complete.

When you arrange an observation, be sure the teacher(s) being observed are doing a capable job. Arrange for someone to talk with the prospect about what was seen.

If you are recruiting for a specific class, it may be helpful to show the prospect the list of children he or she will be working with and describe some of the benefits

of the age level. For example, you might explain that first graders are excited about learning to read and they enjoy being able to locate and read familiar words in their Bible memory verses.

Above all, help prospects realize that no one begins a task in children's ministry with all the required skills.

At least three out of four people want leaders who motivate people to get involved.
Barna Research Group, Ventura, CA 93003. www.barna.org Research Archives: Leadership

Training, experience and support from other teachers—undergirded with God's help—all combine to equip teachers and leaders.

4. Ask the prospect to pray for God's direction in whether or not to accept this commitment and to discuss it with family members. Set a deadline for the prospect's response, usually about one week.

Be prompt in following up with the prospect at the time you agreed upon. This will let the person know that his or her decision is important to you. When the follow-up contact is made, accept the decision given. If the answer is yes, express your appreciation for this new step of commitment. Give the volunteer an application form 💿 to complete and return to you. Be ready to give information about how and when orientation and training will be given to help the new staff member make a good beginning.

If the answer is no, be gracious in thanking the person for having taken the time to explore this ministry. Since you and the prospect both prayed for God's direction in this decision, you can trust the result of His guidance. (It's better that the person withdrew now instead of serving only a few weeks or months with a minimal sense of commitment.) If the person expresses an interest in a different area of ministry, have available the names and phone numbers of other church leaders, so you can connect volunteers with appropriate programs.

Idea Bank

Plan a Coffee and Calling Night. Send an invitation and then follow up with a phone call. Ask several people (current or former teachers) to come to your church office (or another location that has several phone lines). Provide a variety of coffees or teas. Give participants a copy of the recruiting handbook  and a list of potential volunteers to call. Begin and end the evening with a time of prayer. **Tip:** Plan the event on a night when you anticipate prospects are likely to be home (often Monday evenings).

When a large number of teaching positions are to be filled, set up a display in one or more well-traveled areas of your church. A large attractive poster (choose from the posters in *Children's Ministry Recruiting Poster Pack*) will attract attention as will a video or photographs of the program for which you are recruiting. **Tip:** If you want to display a list of jobs to be filled, only do so when you can show that a significant number of positions are already filled. No one wants to be the first to sign up!

Visit adult Sunday School classes or fellowship groups to briefly describe a program for which you are recruiting teachers and leaders. Give each person a small item related to children's ministry (refrigerator magnet, bookmark, etc.). **Tip:** Provide a volunteer response form (often a small card)  which people may complete to indicate their interest in children's ministry.

Make a continuing effort to recruit men for your children's ministry. Ask a male member of your pastoral staff or a current male teacher to write a brief description of how men have been an important part of his spiritual development. Publish the description in a church newsletter or on your church's website, or interview him in a worship service or other all-church event. **Tip:** Set a goal of recruiting at least one man to work in each children's classroom, both for the benefit of children who need positive male role models and to benefit the men themselves.

Give each prospect an item that represents the benefits of teaching children (a small votive candle glued to a poster-board shape with Matthew 5:14—"You are the light of the world"—printed on it, a heart-shaped cookie, a flower, a seed packet or a seedling). **Tip:** Accompany the item with a flier  that encourages the prospect to consider the impact teaching children can make (spreading God's light in the lives of children, sharing love through teaching, helping children to grow).

Give a helium-filled balloon attached to a flier  with a personal note to each person being asked to consider volunteering in children's ministry. Have several people available to distribute the balloons and fliers either as people arrive at church or as the service is dismissed. (Note: Be sure to clear this attention-getting device with other church staff.) Hand-deliver the balloons to the homes of prospects who are missed. **Tip:** Have a few extras ready to give to people who want to know why they're not being given a balloon. Invite them to prayerfully consider volunteering for children's ministry, too.

 If your church presents Bibles to children as part of a worship service, in the presentation include an invitation for people to get involved in support of children's ministry. **Tip:** Have ready an easy volunteer response form for people to use to request further information about teaching.

Combine your recruiting efforts with a child dedication, baptism or confirmation event. Encourage your senior pastor to remind the congregation of the opportunity the church family has to provide spiritual nurture for the youngest members. Invite people to indicate their interest in volunteering for children's ministry. Include in the church bulletin a volunteer response form to complete. **Tip:** Invite all currently involved in teaching children to stand to affirm their commitment to caring for and teaching children.

 Set up a children's ministries booth. Display art or other Bible learning projects done by children. Include a VCR and show a tape of classroom action. Have several children give out recruiting fliers. Prepare sign-up sheets on clip boards or posters mounted on easels. **Tip:** While anyone may come by the booth to find information about children's ministries, send invitations to specific people who you think would be likely prospects for teachers and leaders.

Create a flier that pictures several church staff members as children and as adults. Invite people to become children's ministry teachers and leaders so that they can help teach the leaders of the future. **Tip:** Fliers can be distributed at the end of a worship service or included in a church newsletter.

 Invite one or more members of the congregation to be your prayer partners, praying for the people who will consider joining your ministry. **Tip:** Give a prayer reminder card to each partner.

Develop a recruiting theme  for each year. These themes (slogans and logos) can be used in letters or fliers mailed to preselected prospects, in bulletin or newsletter announcements and in recruiting displays. **Tip:** Supplement printed material by distributing balloons or buttons that show the recruiting theme.

Present a short teacher appreciation or recruiting skit  to the congregation, to an adult Sunday School classes or at a special church event. A skit grabs more attention than a simple verbal announcement. A skit also conveys a sense that the people who work with children are creative and have a good time in what they do. **Tip:** Skits can be done with puppets, with live actors or with a combination of the two.

Create a short recruiting video featuring children in your children's programs. Ask your senior pastor to read the script . Show the video during a worship service, in adult Sunday School classes or at a children's ministry booth. Include information at the end of the video about opportunities for service. **Tip:** Limit the length of the video to three to five minutes so that attention is maintained. (A longer video could be shown at a ministry booth.)

Consider ways to involve people in short-term, nonintimidating ways which may build bridges to further involvement. Ask volunteers to participate in a single children's ministry event (serve food, complete name tags or take photos, etc.). **Tip:** Look for volunteers who may not have had a reason to observe a children's ministry event in action (collegians, singles, seniors, newcomers to your church, etc.).

Publish recruiting ads  in church newsletters, in bulletins and/or on websites. However, when ads such as these are published, people may volunteer who don't meet the qualifications for children's ministry. Be ready to suggest forms of service such as material preparation, supply purchase, bulletin-board decoration, etc. **Tip:** While ads can highlight the needs in children's ministry, they are never a substitute for personal contact and only occasionally will motivate a prospect to offer his or her services.

Jesus said, "Feed my lambs," not "baby-sit" them.

Kids in our church depend on you. They need to know that someone cares. And what better way to show how much you care than by supporting our Children's Ministry team.

Send letters or personalized fliers  to potential volunteers, briefly describing the children's ministry opportunities for which you are recruiting. Follow up the letter with a phone call several days later. **Tip:** Keep letters short and use bullets to highlight the main points. Busy people are unlikely to read a full page of single-spaced copy.

Short-Term Missionary Needed
Location: Children's Ministry
When: Sunday morning
Time: Prayer and preparation during the week
Resources: Curriculum and training
Benefits: Excellent learning opportunity

Screening Procedures

An essential step in the recruiting process is establishing a set of procedures to be followed in screening and approving volunteers. Determine with others in your church the procedures your church will follow to protect both children and volunteers. Consider consulting a legal expert in church liability issues who is familiar with the applicable laws in your state.

Application Forms: Every person who is a volunteer or paid member of your staff should be asked to fill out an application form . Carefully evaluate the information on the form and, if needed, contact the references listed. All applications and reference checks are required to be kept confidential.

Personal Interview: If you are in a large church where people are being contacted who are not well known to others, you may wish to set up an interviewing team of two people to meet with people who have agreed to accept a teaching position. In the interview, review the information on the application form. Talk informally about the person's background and interest in ministry. The purpose of the interview is to get acquainted with the potential teacher so that you are able to assess the person's skills and abilities in a more personal way than in a written statement.

Fingerprinting and Background Checks: Some churches require fingerprinting and police background checks for all staff (paid and volunteer) who work with children. (Check with your local police department or state Department of Justice for information on how such checks are handled in your area.)

Safety Policy: Developing a safety policy form  for preventing and reporting child abuse and endangerment is an important step in the screening process. While a problem is never expected, it is wise to take necessary precautions by developing a written safety policy. All staff should read the safety policy and each year sign a form verifying their compliance with the policy. A safety policy should include

- guidelines for teacher selection (including some or all of the following: application forms, personal interviews, follow-up of references, fingerprinting and criminal-history checks);

- policies to be followed in the classroom and on any church-sponsored outings (number of adults required, name tags, check-in and check-out procedures, rest room guidelines, etc);

- reporting obligations on the part of teachers if child abuse is observed or suspected; and

- step-by-step plans for response to an allegation of child abuse.

Church leaders should approve the safety policy, and all staff familiarized with the policy on an annual basis. It is also recommended that a lawyer evaluate your policy to be sure it conforms to your state's laws regarding the reporting of child abuse. Depending on the kinds of ministry your church provides, you may need to check with your state's social services department to determine licensing laws that apply to church programs such as day care, summer sessions, etc.

It is always best to present the safety policy with an introduction explaining the positive purpose of such a policy: to make your church the best place it can be for the children in your community and to protect teachers should allegations of abuse or child endangerment be made. Provide each children's ministry staff member with a copy of the safety policy and an introductory letter. Regularly provide training for your teachers on appropriate ways to respond to a child's misbehavior.

If someone unknown to you or other members of your church requests to teach or help with children in your ministry, sincerely thank the person for his or her offer. Explain that all staff are required to have regularly attended the church for a minimum of six months to a year (or whatever your church's policy specifies). Be ready to suggest a way the person might help in the program (decorate bulletin boards, be a photographer, help with mailings, etc.) or another area of service in the church until the time requirement has been met.

Term of Service

As life gets busier and busier with seemingly fewer hours in every day, churches continually struggle with recruiting teachers who will serve on a continuing and regular basis. While people serving in support tasks (record keeping, supplies, etc.) may be willing to commit to a year of service, you may experience difficulty in obtaining year-long commitments from people serving as teachers.

Continuity of care is an ideal to strive for constantly. Young children benefit significantly from the security of familiar people in charge of the program. This security creates fewer discipline problems, and more positive learning can take place.

Children aren't the only ones who benefit from consistent teachers. Adults who spend their time teaching children will also find their experience much more enjoyable (and hopefully serve more often) if they are given the opportunity to get to know the children in their classes, learning about each one and appreciating their growth and development.

The ideal plan is to schedule teachers for 12 months at a time. Some churches recruit teachers for the school year, with a different staff for the summer months. Helpers or aides may be asked to commit for terms of one or more consecutive months. (If helpers serve for one month at a time, schedule their terms of service so that they overlap, resulting in some new and some familiar faces each week.)

A system of one-Sunday-a-month teachers or helpers has not proven satisfactory in meeting children's educational and emotional needs, and occasional volunteers never develop a sense of the value of this ministry. The overwhelming attitude in such situations is "I'll take my turn, but don't expect me to like it or to become good at it." In this plan, the coordinator also becomes overwhelmed at the logistics of scheduling, training and distributing materials on a weekly basis.

Step 4:
Make Training the First Step

Beginnings are the most important—and probably the most risky—times for a new recruit, so every possible help to assure his or her success is a must! When a new volunteer makes a commitment to serve on your staff, the training phase of your recruitment program begins. You can't separate recruiting and training; these elements must be linked in order to make your volunteer's experience positive.

Teachers do not automatically know how to guide others in Bible learning. When left untrained, most teachers tend to teach in the way they were taught. Allow new teachers to gain confidence by communicating information to them about teaching methods and program procedures one step at a time.

New Teacher Checklist

❑ Copy of current curriculum materials

❑ Classroom policies and procedures

❑ Names and phone numbers of other teachers

❑ Class schedule

❑ Class roster (including parents' names, addresses and phone numbers)

❑ Building map with restrooms and exits clearly marked

Meet with new leaders and teachers to explain the goals, methods, curriculum and organization of the program in which they will be serving. If you have more than one new staff member, communicate this information in an orientation class. Send an invitation to the class to each new teacher, and follow up with a phone call to encourage attendance.

When meeting with new teachers, review the appropriate job description 🌐. It is helpful to list the specific tasks expected of the teacher. In this list, answer the question, What are the basic things a person should do in order to succeed in this ministry? Include statements explaining why each action is important and how it will benefit the teacher by helping him or her succeed. (For example, "It is important to prepare all materials before the session begins so that you can welcome and greet children as they arrive. Having time to welcome and greet children is a good way to build relationships with and among your class.")

> *Labor at prayer,*
> *then watch God work.*
> *Leaders are trained—not born.*
> Henrietta Mears

Some churches find it helpful to use a contract form 🌐 as part of a new teacher's orientation. Signing these forms highlights the importance of children's ministry.

After the initial orientation of a new teacher, encourage his or her participation in other teacher training events: local, regional or denominational conventions or seminars and regular teachers' meetings. The focus of such training should always be on specific skills the teachers can implement in their next class session.

Idea Bank

Pair each new volunteer with a buddy—a teacher who has been on the job for a while. Encourage the buddy to talk with the new volunteer on a regular basis. (Note: If your existing teachers are not able to model the positive qualities desired, consider grouping new volunteers together and seeking to build them into a supportive team.) **Tip:** Make sure the mentor is familiar with current policies and procedures for your children's ministry.

Use the orientation audiocassette or videocassette provided by your curriculum supplier to acquaint the new teacher or leader with the function of the curriculum. Some churches also provide a simple video that explains to new staff members the procedures of the program, what kind of security exists, application forms, etc. **Tip:** Since volunteers can take home these audiocassettes and/or videos and listen to them or watch them at their leisure, people who can't attend meetings will be able to learn at their own convenience.

Set up a teaching resource table in a resource room. Include videos, articles and/or books of interest to teachers. Teachers are often looking for opportunities to improve their skills. **Tip:** Near the table, post a sign with a slogan that invites people to use the resources and to attend upcoming training sessions (list topics, locations, dates and times).

If a new volunteer is joining a class already in progress, arrange for the new person to observe (provide an observation form ✪) and/or assist an experienced teacher several times. Give the new volunteer a simple assignment or two as a start. Be sure to explain the session plan and how the volunteer's assignment(s) fits into the plan. Increase the areas of responsibility each session as the new worker shows ability and confidence. **Tip:** If the teachers in a class are meeting to plan, invite the new volunteer to attend.

Plan a basic orientation course that presents key topics: how children learn, age characteristics and needs of children, discipline tips, storytelling guidelines, etc. Larger churches may have enough new teachers that they conduct orientation courses as part of their adult education program. **Tip:** Coordinate orientation courses with leaders of other age levels.

Step 5:
Plan Time for Appreciation

Teachers engaged in children's ministry can never receive too much encouragement and appreciation. In fact, while most attention is placed on recruiting new leaders and teachers, an equal amount of attention should be given to keeping the volunteers you've worked so hard to get.

Plan to demonstrate in meaningful ways that your church places a high value on the ministry of teaching children. Also include volunteers who serve in other capacities in your children's ministry.

> *Man builds for a century;*
> *a Sunday School teacher*
> *builds for eternity.*
> Henrietta Mears

In addition to the awards, events and other forms of recognition described in this chapter, offer support to your staff in these ongoing ways.

Plan ahead for substitutes. Agreeing to help in children's ministry should not mean that a person can never take a needed break. Maintain a list of names and phone numbers of people who have already agreed to serve as children's ministry substitutes. In a larger church, one person may need to be the keeper of the list, ensuring that the same people are not called every week. In a smaller church, you may distribute the list to your teachers and helpers themselves, requesting them to notify you or another supervisor whenever a change is made.

Express appreciation. Always be on the lookout for ways to express gratitude to your children's ministry staff in both informal and formal ways.

➤ After a class session, give specific praise to a volunteer for positive actions you observed in the classroom. Praising the volunteer in front of other teachers, the volunteer's family members or parents of children in the volunteer's class will emphasize your appreciation.

➤ Periodically write personal notes of thanks to staff members. Depending on the size of your staff, make a plan to regularly write at least one note each week or month.

➤ Be alert to special times in the lives of your teachers (birthday, job promotion, anniversary, new baby, etc.). The caring you demonstrate for them will model the caring they should show their children.

Event Guidelines

1. **Plan ahead** so that people can arrange their schedules and the event can be well organized.

2. **Mail invitations** and then follow up with a personal call to encourage attendance and to determine the approximate number planning to attend.

3. **Enlist parents of children** and other church members to help plan and lead the event. The more people involved in saying thank-you, the more meaningful the event will be.

4. **Plan a get-acquainted activity** that encourages people to mingle and meet each other.

5. **Keep in mind** that the purpose is to encourage and honor teachers, not to twist their arms to do even more than they've been doing.

Idea Bank

Show the "Thank You" segment from *Volunteer Recruiting Video* (available in *Children's Ministry Recruiting Kit*) as part of a worship service or teacher appreciation event or on a video display set up in a well-traveled area of your church. **Tip:** Publish the names of current teachers in the church bulletin ☻ or on a sign.

Create your own video featuring children and teachers in your children's programs and a script ☻ that expresses appreciation for their efforts. **Tip:** Show the video as part of a teacher appreciation event or a worship service or in an area of the church facility where people congregate before or after worship services.

Present a humorous skit ☻ that extends gratitude to volunteers. **Tip:** Videotape the skit, so it can be shown in a variety of circumstances.

Provide parents and/or children with teacher appreciation fliers ☻ that they can fill in and give to teachers. **Tip:** Collect all the fliers and display them on a poster attached at each teacher's classroom door (make sure each teacher has an equal amount) or on one large poster attached to the wall of a well-traveled hallway.

Display a teacher appreciation poster from *Children's Ministry Recruiting Poster Pack* at a key location at your facility. **Tip:** Reproduce one of the teacher appreciation themes ☻ onto brightly colored paper (enlarge the theme as needed) to make miniposters.

At the beginning or end of the teaching term or school year, give a gift to express appreciation to all teachers. Explain that the gift in no way monetarily reimburses the teacher but that it is a symbol or token of gratitude for faithful, excellent service. Gift ideas can include seasonal ideas (Christmas ornament, spring flowers, etc.), books, coffee mugs, notepads, tote bags, T-shirts, food items (fresh fruit, baked goods, preserves, etc.), gift certificates, class pictures, etc. Gifts that are designed for teacher use every Sunday help create team spirit—for example, a tote bag in which to carry supplies. **Tip:** Some gifts can be imprinted, stenciled, patched or painted with your children's ministry logo ☻.

On a special Sunday (first day of the term, dedication or recognition day, etc.) give each teacher a colorful name tag 🌐 that shows his or her name and how many years he or she has served in children's ministry. **Tip:** Ask teachers to stand during the worship service.

At the end of the teaching term, give each teacher a mini photograph album with pictures of your children's program. **Tip:** Be sure to include several photos that picture the teacher in action.

Let your staff know that their ideas and feedback are appreciated by giving them a feedback form 🌐 to complete at least once a year. Inviting teachers and leaders to give their input assures them of your support. **Tip:** Meet with one or more teachers and/or parents to evaluate the feedback and determine what changes or improvements to make.

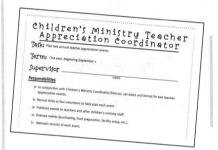

Recruit a person to serve as a coordinator for several teacher appreciation events during the year. Give the coordinator a job description 🌐 and invite him or her to suggest creative ways to express appreciation. **Tip:** A long-time teacher may enjoy this job as a break from serving in the classroom every week.

Ask church members or businesses in your community to donate gift items (gift certificates, books, food items, etc.). **Tip:** Assign a number to each item. During a teacher appreciation event, each volunteer chooses a numbered slip from a container and then receives the item with the matching number.

Once or twice a year (or at the end of a once-a-year program such as Vacation Bible School) invite all staff (and their families) to a special appreciation event 🌐: pizza dinner, build-your-own ice cream sundaes, picnic in the park, brunch, barbecue, etc. You can include a concert, a guest speaker or a video. Teacher appreciation events can be major with decorations, special foods, table centerpieces and entertainment; or they can be low-key and informal. No matter the format of the event, the key is that they be well planned, communicating that someone thinks the teachers are important enough to have gone to some trouble on their behalf. **Tip:** Provide name tags 🌐, especially if you are inviting spouses or children.

Place a sheet of poster board and several felt pens by a classroom door or in the hall near a class. Parents and/or children may write thank-you notes on it. **Tip:** Print a starter sentence or two around the border of the poster board ("I'm glad you're a teacher because . . ." or "Thank you for . . .").

Designate a Sunday at the beginning of the teaching term to dedicate or recognize those who will be teaching in the coming term. You may choose to offer a dedication prayer in the worship service, introduce the teachers and other volunteers in the worship service, or serve special refreshments after church in honor of the teachers who are each given a corsage/boutonniere, button or special name tag 🌐 to wear. Whichever approach you take, be sure to alert the teachers ahead of time, so they are aware of the plan. If your church has multiple worship services, identify which service each teacher will attend. **Tip:** Enlist the pastor to preach on a related topic—importance of ministry to children, the value of service, Jesus as a teacher, etc.

Give a teacher-of-the-month award 🌐 or give each teacher an award 🌐 at the end of the teaching term, at a dedication service or at a teacher recognition event. Ask one or more students from each teacher's class to hand out the awards. **Tip:** Photocopy the awards onto heavy colored paper. They can also be colored with felt pens, glitter pens, etc.

Designate one Sunday as Teacher Treat Day. Ask a parent from each class to bring a basket of muffins or cookies or other treat to the child's teacher. **Tip:** Provide a thank-you flier 🌐 that all children sign.

Invite former students of some of your teachers to write a short article for your church newsletter to publicly thank those who taught them in the past. **Tip:** Ask the student to answer one or more of these questions in the article: Who was one of your favorite teachers? What was something you really liked to do in Sunday School? How did your experiences in children's programs at our church contribute to your understanding of what it means to be a Christian?

Reproducible Resources

All resources are also found on the CD-ROM provided at the back of this book. Use the CD-ROM to customize these resources for your church.

Forms (p. 29)

Job Descriptions (p. 47)

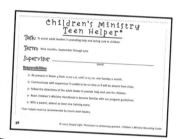

Recruiting (p. 57)

Teacher Appreciation (p. 91)

Forms*

Calendar

Contact Record

Feedback Form

Observation Form

Recruiting Handbook

Safety Policy

Teacher Contract Form

Volunteer Application Form

Volunteer Recommendation Forms

Volunteer Response Forms

Volunteer Survey

*Forms are provided as samples only. Customize each form by using specific information from your church.

Calendar

January	February	March
April	May	June
July	August	September
October	November	December

Contact Record

Name _____

Phone Number _____ Position Opportunity _____

Contact Date _____ By _____

Job Description Given ❑ Yes ❑ No   Follow-Up Date _____

Decision/Comments _____

_____

Application Given ❑ Yes ❑ No   Application Received ❑ Yes ❑ No   Approved ❑ Yes ❑ No

Date Service Begins _____ Date Service Ends _____

Feedback Form

Tell Us What You Think!

Date _____

Name (optional) _____

Describe any concerns you have about our children's ministry. _____

_____

_____

_____

_____

What ideas do you have for improving children's ministry programs?_____

_____

_____

_____

Thank you! Please return form to the church office.

Observation Form

1. What are three characteristics you noticed about the students of this class that are important for a teacher (or other staff member) to keep in mind?

2. List three words that summarize the role of the teacher.

3. What are two ways the teacher (or other staff member) gives individual attention to students?

4. What are two ways the students are involved in discovering Bible truths and hearing and talking about Bible verses or passages?

5. In what ways are students challenged to put Bible truths into practice in their daily lives?

If applicable:

6. What are two ways the lead teacher keeps the session moving smoothly?

7. What are two ways the lead teacher helps the teachers to be successful in their teaching?

Recruiting Handbook
Recruiting Guidelines

1. Begin early!

2. Make sure you have a written job description.

3. Personally contact each prospective volunteer.

Our task in recruiting isn't to nag or manipulate people into service but, rather, to help people thoughtfully consider the very real possibility that God wants to use them to love and teach children. Your recruiting efforts can discover, enlist and lead people who God has already gifted (see Ephesians 4 and 1 Corinthians 12) to make a positive impact on the next generation!

So as you contact and call, keep your eyes on the real goal of recruiting—finding the people God has called to serve Him by fulfilling their God-given potential as teachers and leaders of children.

For we are God's workmanship, created in Christ Jesus to do good works, which God prepared in advance for us to do.
Ephesians 2:10

Recruiting Handbook
Contact Tips

1. Explain why the job is important and why the prospect is considered to have the potential to be effective at the task.

2. Clearly describe the job and what is required to do the job effectively and give a job description.

3. Describe the resources (show samples if meeting in person) and training the church provides. Offer the opportunity for the prospect to observe the ministry before responding.

4. Ask the prospect to pray and respond by a specific date.

Follow-Up Tips

1. Be prompt in following up with the prospect.

2. Accept the decision given. If the answer is yes, express your appreciation. Be ready to give information about how and when orientation and training will be given. If the answer is no, thank the person for having taken the time to consider this ministry.

Recruiting Handbook
Contact List

Name	Phone	Position

Comments

_____

_____

_____

_____

_____

_____

Safety Policy

We desire to protect and support those who work with our children. These policies to prevent child abuse, neglect or any unfounded allegations against workers or teachers address three major areas:

1. Worker selection
2. Worker practices
3. Reporting obligation

SELECTING CHILDREN'S WORKERS

▶ All paid employees, full or part-time, including clergy and all volunteer children's workers should complete a "Volunteer Application Form."

▶ A personal interview will be included as part of the selection process.

▶ Where circumstances merit, personal references listed in the application will be checked to further determine the suitability and character of the applicant. The reference check shall be documented.

▶ All workers with children should normally be members of First Church or have been attending First Church for a minimum of six months.

SAFETY POLICIES FOR CHILDREN'S MINISTRIES

▶ Each group of children should have at least two workers who are not related to each other, at least one being an adult, present at all times.

▶ For children, infant through toddlers, the desirable ratio is one worker for every two or three children. For ages two through kindergarten age, the desirable ratio is one worker for every five children. For grades one through five, the desirable ratio is one worker for each eight children.

▶ Window blinds and doors are to be kept open (or doors should have windows). A supervisor or designated adult representative will circulate where children's activities are occurring.

▶ When taking children to the rest room, workers should supervise children of the same gender. The worker should stay out of the rest room at the open door until the child is finished in the stall. Workers enter to assist only when necessary.

▶ All drivers transporting children on out-of-town activities shall be a minimum age of 25 and maximum age of 65 and shall complete and have approved a "Driver Form."

▶ In the nursery, diapers are to be changed only in designated areas and in the presence of other caregivers.

▶ All youth helpers should be at least four years older than the children they are helping.

REPORTING OBLIGATION AND PROCEDURE

1. All workers are to be familiar with the definitions of child abuse (see below).

2. If a worker suspects that a child has been abused, the following steps are to be followed:

   ▶ Report the suspected abuse to your supervisor.

   ▶ Do not interview the child regarding the suspected abuse. The interview process will be handled by trained personnel.

   ▶ Do not discuss the suspected abuse. It is important that all information about the suspected child abuse (victim and abuser) be kept confidential.

3. Workers reporting suspected child abuse will be asked to complete the Suspected Child Abuse Report (available from your state's Department of Social Services). Confidentiality will be maintained where possible. This report must be completed within 24 hours.

4. Once a suspected child abuse case has been reported by a worker to a supervisor, it will be reported to the designated reporting agency.

DEFINITIONS OF CHILD ABUSE

Defined by The National Committee for Prevention of Child Abuse

Physical Abuse

Nonaccidental injury, which may include beatings, violent shaking, human bites, strangulation, suffocation, poisoning, or burns. The results may be bruises and welts, broken bones, scars, permanent disfigurement, long-lasting psychological damage, serious internal injuries, brain damage, or death.

Neglect

The failure to provide a child with basic needs, including food, clothing education, shelter, and medical care; also abandonment and inadequate supervision.

Sexual Abuse

The sexual exploitation of a child by an older person, as in rape, incest, fondling of the genitals, exhibitionism, or pornography. It may be done for the sexual gratification of the older person, out of a need for power, or for economic reasons.

Teacher Contract Form

I, _____, because I feel called by God, commit to the following guidelines as a Sunday School teacher for the period of _____ to _____. This commitment is reviewable and renewable.

As a teacher, I will

▶ Serve on the teaching team for the _____.

As a teacher, I am committed to Our Lord

▶ I have a personal relationship with Jesus Christ, which I desire to model for children.

▶ I enjoy studying God's Word regularly and desire to grow in my faith and commitment to Him (through personal study, adult classes or home Bible study groups).

Our Church

▶ I worship regularly with our church family.

▶ I support the doctrinal statement and leadership of our church.

My Students

▶ I enjoy children and desire for them to know of God's love and concern for their lives.

▶ I will take the necessary time to prepare my lessons during the week, incorporating my own God-given gifts into each lesson.

▶ I will care for my students individually (through prayer, telephone calls, birthday cards, etc.).

▶ I will be faithful in attendance, arriving at least 15 minutes before the session begins. If I must be absent, I will contact an approved substitute and alert my supervisor.

▶ I will follow up with mailings or visits to absentee class members.

▶ I will participate in at least one training event during the year to improve my teaching skills.

My Teaching Team

▶ I will communicate regularly with my team teachers.

▶ I will participate in scheduled teacher's meetings.

▶ I will care for and return all equipment and curriculum provided.

▶ I will express my needs as a teacher to my supervisor.

_____
Teacher

Volunteer Application Form

First Church has a child safety policy founded on respect and love for the children of our church and community. This safety policy gives children, parents and all children's ministry staff a sense of confidence and peace. We ask cooperation in completing and returning this application.

Personal Information

Name _____ Day and month of birth _____

Address _____

Phone _____ E-mail _____

Best time to call: Morning _____ Afternoon _____ Evening _____

Occupation _____ Where employed _____

Phone _____ Can you receive calls at work? ❑ Yes ❑ No

Do you have a current driver's license? ❑ Yes ❑ No License number _____

Spouse ❑ Yes ❑ No Name _____

Children ❑ Yes ❑ No Name(s) and age(s) _____

Are you currently a member of First Church? ❑ Yes ❑ No If yes, how long? _____

Please list other churches and locations where you have regularly attended over the past five years. _____

_____

_____

Are you currently under a charge or have you ever been convicted of or pled guilty to child abuse or a crime involving actual or attempted sexual misconduct or sexual molestation of a minor? ❑ Yes ❑ No

If yes, please explain. _____

_____

_____

Are you currently under a charge of have you ever been convicted guilty of or pled guilty to possession/sale of controlled substances or of driving under the influence of alcohol? ❑ Yes ❑ No

If yes, please explain. _____

_____

_____

Is there any other information that we should know? _____

_____

_____

_____

Church Activity

1. Please write a brief statement of how you became a Christian.

_____

_____

_____

2. In what activities/ministries of our church are you presently involved?

_____

3. Experience:

    a. What volunteer or career experiences with children have you had in the church or the community?

_____

_____

    b. List any gifts, calling, training, education or other factors that have prepared you for ministry to children.

_____

_____

4. Preferences: In what capacity and with what age group would you like to minister? Explain your choice.

_____

_____

5. Concerns: What causes the greatest feelings of apprehension as you contemplate this ministry?

_____

_____

Personal References   (Not a former employer or relative)

Name _____ Phone _____

Address _____

Name _____ Phone _____

Address _____

Applicant's Statement

The information contained in this application is true and correct to the best of my knowledge. I authorize any of the above references or churches to give you any information that they may have regarding my character and fitness to work with children.

I hereby certify that I have read and that I understand the attached provisions of (insert title of your state's penal code regarding the reporting of child abuse and neglect).

Signature _____ Date _____

Recommendation for Children's Ministry Volunteers

Return form to church office.

I recommend the following person:

Name _____ Phone _____

Address _____

Comments

I feel he/she would _____

_____

_____

_____

_____

Signature _____ Date _____

Recommendation for Teen Helper Volunteers

Return form to church office.

_____ has applied to work as a teen helper

in Children's Ministry.

1. How would you describe this young person's

   ▶ Ability to make friends with young children?

   ▶ Ability to follow adult leadership?

   ▶ Relationship with God?

2. Do you have any reservations about this person's ability to work with young children?

Signature _____ Date _____

Thank you! Your comments will be kept confidential.

Volunteer Response

Name _____ Date _____

Address _____

Phone _____ E-mail _____

Church Member ❏ Nonmember ❏ Age level of interest (if known) _____

(Circle positions of previous service) and underline positions of possible interest:

Department Leader   Teacher

Helper   Substitute Teacher

Secretary   Bulletin Board Decorator

Music (guitar or piano)   Snack Coordinator

Supply Coordinator   Transportation Coordinator

Comments _____

_____

_____

Volunteer Response

I'd like more information about Children's Ministry

❏ so that I can pray for teachers and children.

❏ so that I can pray about helping or serving the children in our church.

Name _____ Date _____

Address _____

Phone _____ E-mail _____

Volunteer Survey

Date _____ Male _____ Female _____

Name _____

Address _____

Phone _____ E-Mail _____

City _____ Zip _____

Occupation _____

Check the appropriate columns: EXP = Experienced (note length); INT = Interested

EXP	INT		EXP	INT	
		Officers/Boards/Committees			**Music**
		Deacon/Deaconess/Elder			Choir member
		Trustee			Soloist
		Facilities			Special group singing
		Christian education			Piano/Organ
		Evangelism			Guitar
		Membership			Keyboard
		Missions			Other instrument
		Finance			Orchestra
		Communications/Media			Children's choir director
		Illustration			Music teacher
		Graphic design			Songleader (age group _____)
		Photography (still/video)			
		Bulletin boards			**Christian Education Positions**
		Lettering			Division coordinator
		Posters			Department leader
		Projectionist			Teacher
		Librarian			Greeter
		Cassette duplication			Helper/Aide/Substitute
		Equipment maintenance			Secretary
		P. A. system			Pianist
		Prepare teaching aids			Recreation leader
		PowerPoint			Resource Center Coordinator

Volunteer Survey (continued)

EXP	INT		EXP	INT	
		Christian Education Programs			Provide meals
		Sunday School			Provide child care
		Churchtime			Entertain visitors at home
		Sunday evening			**Property Maintenance**
		Weekday club			Carpentry
		VBS			Landscaping/Gardening
		Special Education			Painting
		Camp			Electrical
		Christian Education Age Level			Cement work
		Baby/Toddler			Plumbing
		Ages 2 to 5			Custodial
		Grades 1 to 5/6			Mechanical
		Grades 5/6 to 8			**Helpers, Various**
		Grades 9 to 12			Bus driver (license class)
		College			Kitchen cook
		Adults			Kitchen help
		Seniors			Dinners (plan/serve/clean up)
		Outreach			Office/General secretarial
		Home visits/Calling			Typing/Computer
		Discipleship			Filing
		Sick/Shut-in ministry			Telephone
		Men's/Women's ministries			Sewing/Costume design
		Counseling			Photographer
		Ushering/Welcoming/Greeting			Website designer
		Hospitality			
		Home for get-togethers			
		Home for home Bible studies			
		Home for backyard Bible clubs			
		Transportation			
		Loan car/van			
		Lodging			

Job Descriptions

Coordinator/Director

Department Leader/Lead Teacher

Teacher

Others:

Camp Coordinator

Food Coordinator

Greeter

Publicity Coordinator

Recruiting Team Member

Resource Center Coordinator

Teacher Appreciation Coordinator

Teen Helper

Other job descriptions you may wish to create are Children's Choir Director, Club Night Director, Secretary, and Special Events Coordinator.

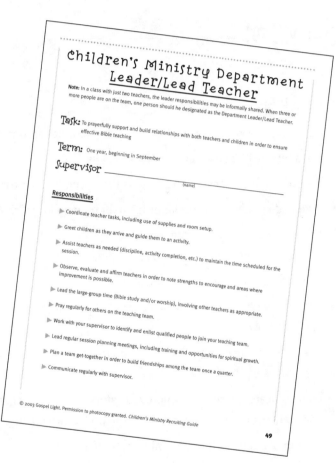

Children's Ministry Department Leader/Lead Teacher

Note: In a class with just two teachers, the leader responsibilities may be informally shared. When three or more people are on the team, one person should be designated as the Department Leader/Lead Teacher.

Task: To prayerfully support and build relationships with both teachers and children in order to ensure effective Bible teaching

Term: One year, beginning in September

Supervisor _____
(name)

Responsibilities

▶ Coordinate teacher tasks, including use of supplies and room setup.

▶ Greet children as they arrive and guide them to an activity.

▶ Assist teachers as needed (discipline, activity completion, etc.) to maintain the time scheduled for the session.

▶ Observe, evaluate and affirm teachers in order to note strengths to encourage and areas where improvement is possible.

▶ Lead the large-group time (Bible study and/or worship), involving other teachers as appropriate.

▶ Pray regularly for others on the teaching team.

▶ Work with your supervisor to identify and enlist qualified people to join your teaching team.

▶ Lead regular session planning meetings, including training and opportunities for spiritual growth.

▶ Plan a team get-together in order to build friendships among the team once a quarter.

▶ Communicate regularly with supervisor.

© 2003 Gospel Light. Permission to photocopy granted. *Children's Ministry Recruiting Guide*

49

Children's Ministry Coordinator/Director*

Note: A church with one or more age-level coordinators may assign some of these responsibilities to those leaders. This leadership role then becomes more one of coordination, encouragement and support.

Task: To guide planning and development of a program of Bible learning for all age levels

Term: One year, beginning in September

Supervisor _____
(name)

Responsibilities

▶ Communicate vision for children's ministry to other groups and leaders within the church

▶ Be familiar with curriculum for all age levels

▶ Recruit leaders, teachers and helpers for all children's programs.

▶ Plan and coordinate a regular program of training for all children's ministry staff.

▶ Observe, evaluate and affirm leaders, teachers and helpers in order to note strengths to encourage and areas where improvement is possible.

▶ Pray regularly for children's ministry staff.

▶ Coordinate regular planning meetings for team members that include training and opportunities for spiritual growth.

▶ Oversee the purchase, distribution and use of all equipment and supplies (curriculum, snacks, art supplies, etc.).

▶ Communicate the church's approved safety policy to all children's ministry staff, regularly evaluate its use and take necessary steps to put the policy into practice.

▶ Lead in planning a children's ministry staff get-together at least twice a year in order to build a sense of teamwork among all teachers.

▶ Express appreciation to children's ministry staff, including an end-of-the-year event.

▶ Communicate with church leaders and the congregation regarding the purpose, value and procedures of children's ministry.

▶ Communicate regularly with leaders of related programs (weekday preschool leader, second-hour coordinator, etc.).

* This position may be held by a volunteer or paid staff person. In a small church, one or more of these tasks may be the responsibility of the pastor, Christian education committee member, children's ministries elder, etc.

Children's Ministry Department Leader/Lead Teacher

Note: In a class with just two teachers, the leader responsibilities may be informally shared. When three or more people are on the team, one person should be designated as the Department Leader/Lead Teacher.

Task: To prayerfully support and build relationships with both teachers and children in order to ensure effective Bible teaching

Term: One year, beginning in September

Supervisor _____
                              (name)

Responsibilities

▶ Coordinate teacher tasks, including use of supplies and room setup.

▶ Greet children as they arrive and guide them to an activity.

▶ Assist teachers as needed (discipline, activity completion, etc.) to maintain the time schedule for the session.

▶ Observe, evaluate and affirm teachers in order to note strengths to encourage and areas where improvement is possible.

▶ Lead the large-group time (Bible study and/or worship), involving other teachers as appropriate.

▶ Pray regularly for others on the teaching team.

▶ Work with your supervisor to identify and enlist qualified people to join your teaching team.

▶ Lead regular session planning meetings, including training and opportunities for spiritual growth.

▶ Plan a team get-together in order to build friendships among the team once a quarter.

▶ Communicate regularly with supervisor.

Children's Ministry Teacher

Task: To prayerfully build relationships with children and guide them in life-changing Bible learning

Term: One year, beginning September 1

Supervisor _____
(name)

Individual Responsibilities

▶ Maintain a personal relationship with Jesus Christ.

▶ Desire to grow in faith and commitment to God and participate in personal Bible study and prayer.

▶ Worship regularly with the church family.

Team Responsibilities

▶ Pray regularly for each child and others on your teaching team.

▶ Participate in scheduled teachers' meetings.

▶ Participate in at least one training event during the year to improve teaching skills.

▶ Express needs as a teacher to your supervisor.

Sunday Morning Responsibilities

▶ Arrange materials and room to create an effective learning environment.

▶ Greet each child upon arrival and involve him or her in conversation and meaningful activity.

▶ Model the love of Christ by getting to know children and sharing their concerns, needs and joys.

▶ Guide Bible learning by

1. being well prepared to use Bible stories, verses/passages, questions and comments appropriate to the age level in order to accomplish the lesson aims;

2. selecting a variety of Bible learning activities and encouraging each student to actively participate in each lesson;

3. participating with children in learning activities and in large-group times.

Student Follow-Up Responsibilities

▶ Follow up on visitors and absentees with mailings, phone calls and/or personal visits.

▶ Care for each class member with prayer, telephone calls, birthday cards, etc.

▶ Communicate individual student needs to parents.

Children's Ministry Camp Coordinator

Task: To plan and reserve summer and/or winter camp reservations, publicize the camp program and oversee all details (counselors, registration, transportation, etc.)

Term: One year, beginning September 1

Supervisor _____
(name)

Responsibilities

▶ In coordination with supervisor, reserve date and number of campers at (name of camp). Coordinate camp dates with school schedules.

▶ Request and display camp brochures in the appropriate children's ministry rooms and in other well-traveled areas of the church facility.

▶ Write bulletin notices for camps and send publicity materials with parent letters well in advance of registration due dates.

▶ Set up and oversee procedures for accepting registrations and fees.

▶ Mail all checks and registration material to the camp registrar.

▶ Plan and coordinate scholarships and fund-raisers as needed.

▶ Two weeks prior to camp, send an information letter to each camper. Include information about final payment of all camp fees, transportation arrangements, luggage, address at camp, medical release forms, etc.

▶ After camp, ask several campers to write an article for church newsletter and/or arrange for several campers to be interviewed during church service.

▶ Communicate regularly with supervisor.

Children's Ministry Food Coordinator

Task: To oversee the provision of food—snacks or meals—as needed at Sunday School and related children's programs

Term: One year, beginning September 1

Supervisor _____
(name)

Responsibilities

▶ Determine the food needs for all children's programs, working with children's ministry teachers.

▶ Provide food through purchases and donations of money or food. If parents are asked to provide food, set up and oversee a schedule of donations.

▶ Recruit cooks as needed.

▶ Keep records of and help teachers be informed about food allergies.

▶ Set guidelines for food handling and cleanup.

Children's Ministry Greeter

Task: To greet families and check in children as they arrive for Sunday School

Term: Six months, September through February

Supervisor _____
(name)

Responsibilities

▶ Be present in the classroom 15 minutes before program begins and stay 15 minutes after the start of the program each Sunday morning.

▶ Put out a new check-in form each Sunday. Place previous check-in form into the Attendance Form box in the reception office.

▶ Assist parent(s) as needed to check in.

▶ Offer a friendly greeting to each family, alerting families to any special announcements or procedural changes.

▶ Pay special attention to guests. Get names and addresses, give name tags, direct children and parents to appropriate rooms, etc.

▶ Communicate regularly with supervisor.

Children's Ministry Publicity Coordinator

Task: To communicate information about Sunday School and related children's programs and events

Term: One year, beginning September 1

Supervisor _____
(name)

Responsibilities

▶ Determine the ongoing publicity needs for all children's programs, including mailed publicity, displays at church, bulletin and/or newsletter inserts, videos, etc.

▶ Oversee the production and distribution of all children and parent letters, fliers, posters, etc., working with others as needed (office staff, children's leaders, etc.).

Children's Ministry Recruiting Team Member

Task: With a team of three or four others, recruit volunteers for open children's ministry staff positions

Term: Three months, March through May

Supervisor _____
(name)

Responsibilities

▶ Meet twice a month with the recruiting team to prepare, plan and pray.

▶ Contact by phone or personal visit potential children's ministry volunteers, following the recruiting guidelines (see "Recruiting Handbook").

▶ Follow up each contact within a week.

▶ Report results of contacts to team members.

Children's Ministry Resource Center Coordinator

Task: To keep the resource center organized and ready for teacher use

Term: Six months, September through February or March through August

Supervisor _____
(name)

Responsibilities

▶ Once a week, check the resource center to clean up and sort donated materials and pick up supply requests submitted by teachers.

▶ Purchase supplies as needed. Consult with Children's Ministry Coordinator/Director as needed. Turn in receipts to (name).

▶ Place supply requests for donated items in church newsletter and/or bulletin as needed.

▶ Keep a current copy of appropriate supply and equipment catalogs.

▶ Update supply list twice a year, post list in the resource center and distribute to teachers.

▶ At least twice a year, thoroughly clean and reorganize the resource center.

▶ Communicate regularly with supervisor.

Children's Ministry Teacher Appreciation Coordinator

Task: Plan two annual teacher appreciation events

Term: One year, beginning September 1

Supervisor _____
(name)

Responsibilities

▶ In conjunction with Children's Ministry Coordinator/Director, set dates and format for two teacher appreciation events.

▶ Recruit three or four volunteers to help plan each event.

▶ Publicize events to teachers and other children's ministry staff.

▶ Oversee events (purchasing, food preparation, facility setup, etc.).

▶ Maintain records of each event.

Children's Ministry Teen Helper*

Task: To assist adult leaders in providing help and loving care to children

Term: Nine months, September through June

Supervisor _____
(name)

Responsibilities

▶ Be present in Room 4 from 11:00 A.M. until 12:15 P.M. one Sunday a month.

▶ Communicate with supervisor if unable to be on time or if will be absent from class.

▶ Follow the directions of the adult leader to provide help and care for children.

▶ Read *Children's Ministry Handbook* to become familiar with our program guidelines.

▶ With a parent, attend at least one training event.

*Teen helpers must be recommended by church youth leaders.

Recruiting

Skits and Video Script*

Themes

*Skits and videos can be presented during worship services, adult classes or special church events.

Act It Out

The following skit requires audience participation. Make sure the actors you use are very animated and enthusiastic in order to get the audience involved.

Choose as many of the following sayings about teachers as you have time for. One or two actors lead the audience in playing Charades, acting out the different words as the audience guesses what the word is. The actors may use motions, numbers, signals or act out scenes, but they should not use words or sounds. As the words are correctly guessed, a leader writes the words on a large sheet of paper. Continue until someone calls out the complete saying. (Optional: Write each saying on a large sheet of paper, leaving blank lines for three or four words that can be easily acted out. Actors lead audience in guessing the missing words. As each missing word is guessed, audience suggests where it should be written. Continue until all sayings are identified.)

Choose from the following sayings:

▶ What you teach them now will teach them forever.

▶ Jesus said, "Feed my lambs."

▶ Love a child. Touch the future. (For the word "future," divide the word into syllables and act out "Phew!"—as if something smells bad—and "chair.")

▶ Pass it on!

▶ To teach a child is to know the joy of giving.

▶ Train a child in the way he should go.

Introduce the Charades activity by saying, "Let's see if you can figure out a reason why children's ministry is so valuable." After one or more sayings have been guessed, conclude by saying, "That's right! (Repeat the sayings.) Our children's ministry staff believes we make an impact on the lives of the children in our church. You can join our team by contacting (name of contact person) at (time and place)."

A Conversation with Moses

Children's Leader:	*(Enters.)* Hi, everyone. I'm here today to talk about how you can become a leader in our children's ministry programs. But first I thought we'd meet one of the Bible's all-time great leaders: Moses!
Moses:	*(Enters, wearing Bible-times clothing and carrying his staff. He answers humbly and seems a bit embarrassed.)* Thank you.
Children's Leader:	Moses, we're hoping some people will volunteer to lead in our children's ministry programs. We'd like to hear about your life as a leader.
Moses:	Well, I didn't exactly volunteer. In fact, I tried to get out of it! I kept trying to explain to the burning bush—
Children's Leader:	*(Interrupting.)* Burning bush?
Moses:	That's right. God spoke to me from a burning bush.
Children's Leader:	Well, folks, that's one special effect you won't get from me! Moses, please continue.
Moses:	The first thing I asked was "Why me?"
Children's Leader:	I'll bet there are people here who are thinking the same thing when it comes to children's ministry. *Why me? What do I have to offer kids?* What did God say to you?
Moses:	God promised to be with me.
Children's Leader:	Wow! What a great promise! God promises the same thing to our teachers. You must have felt really good to know God would be with you.
Moses:	I probably should have felt good. God even told me to tell the Israelites that the God of Abraham, Isaac and Jacob had sent me.
Children's Leader:	So after God gave you His authority to speak to the Israelites, and knowing He would be with you, you must have been raring to go!
Moses:	Uh . . . nope.
Children's Leader:	*(Incredulously.)* "Nope"?
Moses:	I was worried they'd call me a liar and say that God never appeared to me.
Children's Leader:	*(Staring at him, stupefied.)* You *are* Moses, the famous leader, aren't you? The man who wrote the first five books of the Bible? The man who led the Israelites out of captivity in Egypt? You are THAT Moses . . . right?

Moses:	*(Smiling apologetically.)* Uh . . . yeah. That's me.
Children's Leader:	It's hard to believe such a great leader could have so many doubts. But then again, there may be great leaders sitting in the congregation right now who can't believe they'd be any good leading our kids, too.
Moses:	I was positive that I was NOT the right person for the job. After all, I've never considered myself a great speaker and a leader has to be someone who can speak well in front of people.
Children's Leader:	But since God was the one who asked you to do the job, didn't you think He would give you all the help you would need?
Moses:	I didn't really think of it that way. In fact, I finally just asked God to find someone else to do the job!
Children's Leader:	*(Sadly.)* I hear that all the time myself.
Moses:	It's pretty embarrassing to admit. Especially since everyone usually thinks of me as such a strong and powerful leader. But it really wasn't me at all. I didn't want the job! It was God working through me. And it was GREAT to see all the wonderful things He did! God can work through others, too! I hope no one misses out on the good things God can do when we answer His call.
Children's Leader:	Thank you, Moses. Some of you will be contacted in the next few weeks by our children's ministry team. We've been praying about the people God can use in teaching and loving kids. So don't look for any burning bushes, but do watch for a letter from (name of contact person). And if you already feel that God is nudging you to participate in children's ministry, please see (name of contact person) at (time and place). *(Children's Leader and Moses exit.)*

A Series of Brief Encounters

The following three skits can be performed individually, or collectively as one long skit. If you choose to perform all three at one time, change the dialogue as needed for smooth transitions.

Encounter 1: Mr. Goodsport

Children's Leader: *(Enters, carrying clipboard and pen. Speaks to audience.)* Hi, there. I'm sorry I haven't really got time to talk now. I've got several people I need to see. *(Starts to move on and then turns back to audience.)* I need to see them about getting involved in our children's ministry. Oh, here comes one of the people on my list now.

Mr. Goodsport: *(Enters carrying golf clubs, tennis racket, fishing pole, etc. He's singing perhaps off-key but enthusiastically.)* Heigh-ho, heigh-ho, the weekend's here you know. There's golf and tennis and fishing and fun, heigh-ho, heigh-ho, heigh—

Children's Leader: *(Interrupts.)* Excuse me, Mr. Goodsport. I'm glad I ran into you. I've been wanting to talk to you about that letter you received from our children's ministry team.

Mr. Goodsport: Letter? Letter? Oh, letter! . . . Later. I'm on my way to a weekend full of activity. Can you catch me some other time? *(Continues on his way, still singing.)* Heigh-ho, heigh-ho—

Children's Leader: *(Interrupts.)* But I wanted to talk to you about the children.

Mr. Goodsport: *(Stops, turns back to* Children's Leader.*)* The children? Oh, yes, the children. I'm sorry, but expecting me to be in church every Sunday to baby-sit some children is just out of the question. It's too bad Sunday comes on a weekend. Oops, gotta run. It's later than I thought. *(Exits, singing.)* Heigh-ho, heigh-ho . . .

Children's Leader: But Mr. Goodsport . . . *(To audience.)* He was in such a hurry, I didn't have time to tell him we have a regular substitute for that class. So on the occasional weekend when a teacher needs to be gone, the substitute can step in. Maybe I can catch up with him on the eighteenth green. *(Exits.)*

Other Leader: I hope (s)he does catch up with Mr. Goodsport. He's filled his life so full of activity, he hasn't left room for ministry. That means he's really missing out! I trust none of you will let this next year slip by without finding the deep satisfaction of serving God and others—perhaps by teaching children.

Encounter 2: Mrs. Past Tense

Children's Leader: *(Enters, looking at clipboard, making marks with pen, talking to self.)* Who haven't I talked to yet about our children's ministry? Saw him. Found her. Saw her. Found him. Here's one! *(Looks up.)* And here she comes!

Mrs. Past Tense: *(Enters enthusiastically and waves.)* There you are. I've been looking all over for you.

Children's Leader: What a coincidence—I was looking for you.

Mrs. Past Tense: Thank you for thinking of me with that lovely letter about the children.

Children's Leader: That's why I was looking for you, to find a time when I could share with you some of the exciting things happening with children in our church.

Mrs. Past Tense: Oh, that would be lovely. But, of course, you know I did my turn with Sunday School when my children were young. I'll never forget those years. But now . . .

Both: *(In unison.)* It's someone else's turn.

Mrs. Past Tense: I'm so glad you agree with me. It's so good of you to put up with those noisy, wiggly kids. I'm so glad I don't have that responsibility any more. *(Waves as she exits.)* Keep up the good work!

Children's Leader: *(To audience, sadly.)* That's too bad. Her energy and enthusiasm really reached through to the kids. *(Slowly writes on clipboard.)* "It's someone else's turn." *(Looks up.)* The Bible doesn't say anything about taking turns with ministry. And once you've done a good deed, you don't become exempt! God's blessings for the people who serve His children just keep on coming!

Mrs. Past Tense: *(Returns.)* Oh, good! You're still here! *(Pauses and continues thoughtfully.)* I was just remembering how good it felt to see children's eyes light up when they learn something new. I miss that! I'd love to help. Where do you need me?

Children's Leader: Oh, good! I wanted to tell you about a brand-new teacher who would love to have a partner with your skills and experience. *(They exit together as* Children's Leader *continues explaining.)* You'd not only be loving and teaching some wonderful children, but you'd also be helping us develop a whole new generation of teachers!

Other Leader: Who really is responsible for the children of our church and our community? Maybe Mrs. Past Tense—and all of us—need the message of Proverbs 3:27: "Do not withhold good from those who deserve it, when it is in your power to act."

Encounter 3: Mr. N. Vert

Children's Leader: *(Enters, carrying clipboard and pen. Speaks to audience.)* There's just one person left on my list. Some really great people have accepted the challenge to be part of the children's ministry team. But I haven't been able to find Mr. Vert. Has anyone seen Mr. N. Vert around?

Member: *(From back row of audience.)* He's back here!

Children's Leader: Back there? Oh, I see him. Mr. Vert! Hi!

Mr. Vert: *(Gets up from back row, comes forward shyly, hands in pockets or clasped in front.)* Well, I've sort of been keeping a low profile.

Children's Leader: Why is that?

Mr. Vert: Ever since I got that letter from the children's ministry team, I've been avoiding all of you.

Children's Leader: Avoiding us?

Mr. Vert: I hoped if you didn't see me around, you'd sort of forget you sent me the letter and then I wouldn't have to invent an excuse not to help out with the children's programs.

Children's Leader: Invent an excuse?

Mr. Vert: *(Looks around.)* Is there an echo in here?

Children's Leader: *(Also looks around.)* An echo in here? *(Turns to* Mr. Vert.*)* You don't have to invent excuses. We're not trying to twist anyone's arm. We sent you that letter because we feel you have a lot to offer our children.

Mr. Vert: Oh, I'm sure there are many people who could do much better than I could. I'm not really the type for teaching kids.

Children's Leader: I'm not sure there is a type for teaching kids. But I do know that someone as friendly and caring and thoughtful as you are is someone who can benefit children.

Mr. Vert: Do you think so? But I've never taught before. I've never done ANYTHING like that before.

Children's Leader: Would you be willing to visit a class and see what goes on—to help you get an idea of what you could do to make a difference for some children?

Mr. Vert: Make a difference? Me? Do you really think I could make a difference?

Children's Leader: *(Starts to exit along with* Mr. Vert.*)* I'm sure you could make a big difference. Which of the next three Sundays would be the best time for you to observe a class in action? *(Exits.)*

Other Leader: You may not be as shy as Mr. N. Vert, but you may never have had the exciting privilege of making a real difference in someone's life either. Our children's ministry team is looking for some friendly, loving, thoughtful people who want to make a positive difference. (Explain how to express an interest in children's ministry.)

Kid Talk

Videotape a variety of children from your church as they answer several questions about children's ministry programs. Be sure to include kids from a variety of age levels. Choose from the following questions and/or write some of your own to fit the programs you offer:

▶ What is your favorite thing to do at Sunday School?

▶ What are some of the other things you do at Sunday School?

▶ What is the funniest thing that ever happened at Sunday School?

▶ What is your teacher like?

▶ What kinds of songs do you sing? Would you sing one of the songs?

▶ What do you think God is like?

▶ What do you know about Jesus?

▶ What's your favorite Bible story? What happens?

▶ Why do you think God wants us to know that story?

Include a short introduction and conclusion to the video.

Introduction: Every Sunday the children in our church family gather together for times of Bible exploration and discovery. Listen in on some of their ideas.

Conclusion: We are thankful for the people who participate in the nurturing of our church's most valued resource—our children. We welcome your help as a prayer partner, a teacher, a helper—but most of all as a friend and example. (Explain how to express an interest in children's ministry.)

Locked Out

Children's Leader: I had the worst dream last night! I dreamt that NONE of our teachers showed up on Sunday. The doors were locked and the classrooms were empty! Can you imagine?

(Wearing Bible-times costumes, Deborah and Peter enter from opposite sides of the stage. Children's Leader stands to one side of stage.)

Peter: *(Waving.)* Why, Deborah! It's good to see you.

Deborah: Hi, Peter! What are you doing here?

Peter: I came today because the third- and fourth-graders were going to hear a Bible story about me. And you?

Deborah: I came for the 4- and 5-year-old class. I guess the same thing happened to you that happened to me.

Both: *(In unison.)* Nobody showed up to teach. *(They shake their heads.)*

Peter: I saw several parents walk up to the classroom and try the door, but since it was locked, they just took their kids and walked away.

Deborah: Same here. It's too bad. If someone had shown up to teach, the kids would have heard about God's power and how He delivered Sisera's army to the Israelites.

Peter: Oooo! That's a GREAT story! I remember hearing that one myself when I was a boy. God told you to tell Barak to take 10,000 men up Mount Tabor, but Barak was afraid to go without you. You knew you could trust God, so you went with them. *(Dramatically, using motions as he retells the story.)* And God sent a terrific thunderstorm! Sisera's army got their chariots stuck in the mud! *(He laughs heartily.)* Barak's army chased them until there was no one left to chase!

Deborah: That's right. The kids would have learned that we won the battle because we obeyed God. They would know that they can learn about God's Word and obey Him, too. *(Pauses.)* Say, Peter, you had some wonderful adventures with Jesus. Which one were the kids going to learn about?

Peter: It's kind of an embarrassing story, but they were going to learn about the time I walked on the water with Jesus—

Deborah:	*(Interrupting.)* Oh yes! You ended up ALL WET in that one! *(She laughs.)*
Peter:	*(Laughing along good-naturedly.)* I sure did! But that's what I deserved for not trusting Jesus to take care of me. I got scared, and down in the water I went! Still, even though I made a mistake, when I called out to Jesus, He helped me. I'm just sorry no kids got to learn that lesson. Everyone needs to know that Jesus loves and helps us.
Deborah:	*(Nodding sadly.)* Let's just hope someone shows up next week to teach.
Peter:	I agree!
	(Deborah *and* Peter *walk off together.*)
Children's Leader:	I was so relieved when I woke up and realized that my nightmare could never come true in our church. God has given us faithful, dedicated people who make teaching God's Word a priority. If you'd like to join our great team, please see (name of contact person) at (time and place).

My Most Embarrassing Moment by Bartholomew the Disciple

Bartholomew: *(Enters wearing Bible-times clothing.)* Hi! *(Waves.)* My name is Bartholomew and I am one of Jesus' followers. I think you folks call my friends and me disciples. We knew Jesus personally!

You know, Jesus was a pretty radical teacher! I can't tell you how many times we were with Jesus and we THOUGHT we knew the right thing to do, but then Jesus showed us what God REALLY wanted us to do. I remember one time . . . well, this is pretty embarrassing, but we really learned a lot that day.

We'd been traveling with Jesus for a while and everywhere we went, people would come from EVERYWHERE to talk to Him. Once, Jesus had been teaching for several hours—for several days—and my friends and I knew He must have been exhausted. Suddenly, all these PARENTS showed up and brought their KIDS with them! I just knew the last thing Jesus needed was a bunch of wiggly, grubby, noisy KIDS!

(Indignantly.) So Peter, Matthew and I, along with the others, decided enough was enough. We told those parents to take their kids and GO AWAY! How rude for them to interrupt Jesus' important work and irritate Him with . . . KIDS!

(Thoughtful pause.) But Jesus had an entirely different take on the situation. *(Chuckles softly.)* As a matter of fact, Jesus was irritated, but He was irritated with US! Jesus said, "Let the little children come to me, and do not hinder them, for the kingdom of God belongs to such as these."* Whoa! We couldn't believe it! Here we were thinking the kids were just a pain to be dealt with, and Jesus was telling us that the kids were every bit as important as any adult was. In fact, the next thing Jesus said was, "I tell you the truth, anyone who will not receive the kingdom of God like a little child will never enter it."**

Man, I'd never heard ANYTHING like that before! Adults are supposed to be like children? It was amazing. Then Jesus stopped, took the children into His arms and blessed them. You see, to Jesus, the children were worthy of His time and attention.

That's a day I'll never forget. Thanks for letting me share with you about my most embarrassing moment. Well, . . . most embarrassing so far. *(Bartholomew exits.)*

Children's Leader: Jesus loved children and we love children, too! If you'd like to learn more about the different ministries we have available for children please see (name of contact person) at (place and time).

*Mark 10:14   **Mark 10:15

Quiz Show

This skit requires five well-known and respected leaders of your congregation who can be good sports about being foils for a puppet (Sally). Insert the titles and names of these church staff members or other leaders, and adapt the information about the various children's ministries to fit those that you offer.

Emcee: We are proud to present an exciting contest of Bible knowledge: featuring the members of our church staff: our pastor, Youth Director, Music Director, office secretary and a board member—against a typical child from our children's ministries. That sounds about even. So, staff, are you ready?

Staff: *(Ad-libbing: "Yo!" "Right on!" "Let's do it!")*

Emcee: Sally, are you ready?

Sally: I sure am!

Emcee: The first question is for our pastor. After the battle of Jericho, where did Joshua bury the survivors?

Pastor: The Dead Sea? Get it? The DEAD Sea?

Emcee: Try again, Pastor.

Pastor: (Name of a local cemetery)?

Emcee: Sorry, Pastor. Sally, do you know where Joshua buried the survivors of the battle of Jericho?

Sally: Nowhere. You don't bury survivors!

Emcee: Correct! One point for Sally—and our next question is for our Youth Director. Who was the shortest man in the Bible?

Youth Director: Zacchaeus? The little man who climbed the tree to see Jesus?

Emcee: Sorry. Sally, who was the smallest man in the Bible?

Sally: That's easy! Bildad the Shuhite. Get it? Shoe-height!

Staff: *(All groan in unison.)*

Emcee: Right again! You have two points, Sally. Let's see how our Music Director can do on this next question. How many animals did Moses take on the ark?

Music Director: According to Genesis 6 and 7, he took two of each species that was considered unclean and seven pairs of every clean species.

Emcee:	Sorry. Sally?
Sally:	MOSES didn't take any animals on the ark. NOAH did!
Emcee:	You're on a roll, Sally. Let's see how our office secretary does with this next question. Where was Abraham when the lights went out?
Secretary:	Egypt? Haran? Hebron? Mount Sinai?
Emcee:	Good try. Sally, do you know where Abraham was when the lights went out?
Sally:	In the dark!
Emcee:	Boy, you're sharp today, Sally. Let's see if one of our board members can win this last point for the staff. Who were the first three men Jesus chose to be His epistles?
Board Member:	Peter, James and John.
Emcee:	I'm really sorry. Sally?
Sally:	Jesus didn't choose ANY epistles. He chose APOSTLES!
Emcee:	Wow, Sally, how did you get so smart?
Sally:	Well, I never miss Sunday School every Sunday morning at (time).
Emcee:	Are all the kids who come to Sunday School this smart?
Sally:	Oh, no! I'm the smartest!
Emcee:	I see.
Sally:	I'm also the best singer in the children's choir that practices on (day and time).
Emcee:	I see.
Sally:	And I graduated with highest honor from the church preschool.
Emcee:	I see.
Sally:	And I win more awards than anyone at VBS every summer.
Emcee:	I see. Anything else we should know about you?
Sally:	Besides my naturally curly hair?
Emcee:	Besides that.
Sally:	And my captivating smile?
Emcee:	Not counting that.
Sally:	Well, I'm also very good at being humble.

Emcee: *(To audience.)* Not all of the kids who participate in our children's ministries are as exceptional as Sally, but they are all very special to God—and to us. If you're a parent, one of the best things you can do for your child is to bring him or her regularly to Sunday School every Sunday morning and to children's choir on (day and time). *(To Sally.)* Sally, is there anything you'd like to say to all these nice people about our children's ministries?

Sally: I thought you'd never ask. *(To audience.)* I'd just like to say, we need grown-ups like you to be our friends, to learn our names and say "Hi" when we run—I mean when we WALK—past you.

Emcee: Good idea, Sally.

Sally: And we need some of you to be our special friends on Sunday morning in Sunday School or in our children's music programs.

Emcee: Thank you, Sally.

Sally: *(Getting louder.)* So before you leave, talk to (name)—she's the lady who leads the children's choir or look for (name)—he's the man who schedules teachers and helpers. Find out how you can be a special friend to a child this year!

Emcee: *(To audience.)* I guess she said it all. Thank you!

Help Kids Walk with Jesus!

Nurture God's Children

Serving Children with Joy

Learning for Life
Be a Teacher

Our Kids Are Counting on You

Teach a Child. Grow a Life.

Complete the Circle— Teach Our Children

Reach Out!

Teach a child.

Pass it on!

Love a Child. Touch the Future.

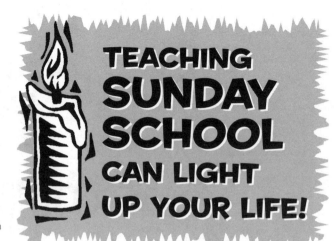

TEACHING SUNDAY SCHOOL CAN LIGHT UP YOUR LIFE!

ADMIT ONE

☞ RESERVED FOR YOU ☜

PrimeTime For Kids

A unique and exciting opportunity to share Jesus' love with children.

"Teach a child in the way he should go, and when he is old he will not turn from it."
Proverbs 22:6

Make a difference in Children's Ministry.

OPEN UP YOUR HEART
TO A CHILD'S LOVE!

Let the children come.

More than diapers and toys! The ministry of the nursery touches lives for eternity.

What will your contribution be? Be a part of our teaching team and give your faith away.

Show You Care! Join our team in Children's Ministry!

Worried about the future? Begin today to teach a child.

Short-Term Missionary Needed

Location: Children's Ministry

When: Sunday morning

Time: Prayer and preparation during the week

Resources: Curriculum and training

Benefits: Excellent learning opportunity

Join our Children's Ministry team!

You'll never look at children the same way again.

Hands Across the Years

You Can Bridge the Gap

We Like Your Smile!

Share It with a Child!

Show You Care!

HIDE 'N SEEK

WE'RE

SEEKING

A FEW GOOD PEOPLE TO HELP KIDS

HIDE

GOD'S WORD IN THEIR HEARTS.

A promise to be an example.

A promise to listen.

A promise to be a friend.

Be a promise keeper in Children's Ministry.

You can be the light in a child's life.

The Children's Ministry Team needs you.

Stand by Me

Did You Know?

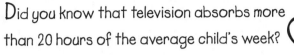

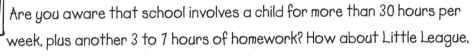

Did you know that television absorbs more than 20 hours of the average child's week? Are you aware that school involves a child for more than 30 hours per week, plus another 3 to 7 hours of homework? How about Little League, which often requires 5 or more hours per week? Or music lessons, which take up 2 to 4 hours per week? Then there's the church. It averages less than 1 hour per week of effective personal and spiritual guidance.

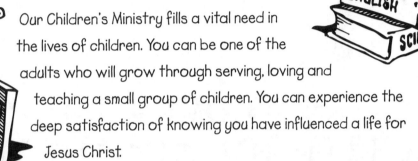

Our Children's Ministry fills a vital need in the lives of children. You can be one of the adults who will grow through serving, loving and teaching a small group of children. You can experience the deep satisfaction of knowing you have influenced a life for Jesus Christ.

Some people come into our lives and go quickly. Some stay awhile and leave footprints in our hearts, and we are never, ever the same!

A child needs you to be the special person in his or her life.
Our church needs you to support Children's Ministry.

WHAT CAN A PERSON DO THAT:

Was specifically applauded by Jesus ("Let the little children come to me" —Mark 10:14)?

Makes a positive difference over a full life span as well as for eternity?

Touches, not just an individual, but a whole family?

Nurtures you more than it does the one you help?

Helps you stay young at heart?

YOU CAN BECOME A PART OF OUR CHILDREN'S MINISTRY TEAM!

So what's a Christian anyway?

We Owe Our Kids an Explanation.

Sunday School helps kids learn the basics of becoming a Christian and living as God's child.

We need you to join our team of Sunday School teachers.

When we're dealing with something as important as the faith of our kids, we owe them that much.

Top 5 Reasons to Join Our Nursery Staff

5. Smiles are given away for free.

4. You'll see kids growing right before your very eyes.

3 Babies and toddlers will think anything you do, say or sing is perfect.

2. You'll make lots of friends.

1. And the number one reason to join our nursery staff:

You'll be following Jesus' example of welcoming children to the family of God!

Help our little ones get the big picture of God's love through the little things of everyday life!

SIDE BY SIDE

COME ALONG AND JOIN OUR CHILDREN'S MINISTRY TEAM!

Touch the hand of a little one!

We've heard that you'd be a good person to help us provide safe and loving care for the children in our nursery.

Hands-on opportunities for ministry in the nursery include giving hugs, playing with toys, clapping hands, turning the pages of a book and giving happy smiles! We hope that you can give us a hand!

Plant a seed of faith!

Lots of little plants are waiting to be cared for in our nursery. You have been recommended as someone who is capable of helping a little child grow by joining our team of faithful "gardeners."

- ☀ I'd love to be a gardener in the nursery!

- ☀ I can't be a gardener in the nursery right now (but call me in a few months).

- ☀ I'm gardening in a different plot right now!

I prefer to work in the garden of the
☀ Seedlings(Babies) ☀ Sprouts (Toddlers) ☀ Any garden is fine!

Jesus said, "Feed my lambs," not "baby-sit" them.

Kids in our church depend on you. They need to know that someone cares. And what better way to show how much you care than by supporting our Children's Ministry team.

"And he took the children in his arms, put his hands on them and blessed them." Mark 10:16

Will you help Jesus bless another child?

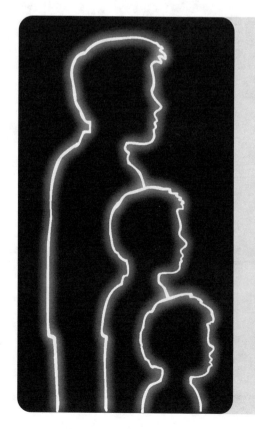

What you teach them now will teach them forever.

Become a part of our Children's Ministry team. Your efforts will have a lifetime effect.

Everybody talks about "kids these days."

Now you can do something about it.

Right now, you can join others who are committed to communicating God's Word to children. We need your support for our Children's Ministry.

Plant a seed. Grow a tree. Teach a child. Grow a life.

Help our kids connect

"O God, give me time to tell this new generation about all your mighty miracles." (See Psalm 71:18.)

Take time this year to teach children.

The world children live in has changed.

The need for teachers has not.

Help share God's Word in today's world. Join our Children's Ministry team.

Here's What We Need to Build Our Nursery Staff!

Caregivers
Sit on the floor
Sing songs and tell stories
Give TLC to show
God's love

Decorator
Good with masking tape
Can design
bulletin boards
Looks at life from
a child's view

Supply Coordinator
Makes lots of lists
Drives to the store
Purchases diapers
and graham crackers

Greeter
Has big smile
Gives encouraging
words
Talented with
name tags

We'll give you everything you need.

Our kids need everything you have to give!
Join our team of volunteers.

Teacher Appreciation

Awards

Events

Name Tags

Skits and Video Script*

Themes

*Skits and videos may be presented during worship services, adult classes or teacher appreciation events.

All-Star Teacher

_____

Certificate of Merit

This certificate is Presented to

_____

in recognition of outstanding service
in Children's Ministry at

_____

_____
Signature

Thanks for helping our kids
Grow in God's Word!

Children's Ministry

Blue-Ribbon Award to

_____

for

_____

Teacher—

You Are Special!

Dear _____

My mommy told you thank-you today for taking care of me. I wish I could talk, too! Here's what I would say.

I'm glad you noticed how much fun I was having playing with the blocks! First, I built towers. But then I banged the block on lots of things—the ball, the car, the wall and even your leg! (I'm sorry that hurt you. Thanks for giving me a train to bang on instead!) You let me figure out how a block works! I learned a lot!

Whenever I come into the room, you smile at me. It makes me feel so good to see you! Sometimes I'm a little sad that my mom is leaving, so I can't smile back. But deep inside, I know you care for me. Thank you.

I heard you talk about Jesus today. I don't exactly know who He is, but if He loves me as much as you do, He must be pretty special! I love you!

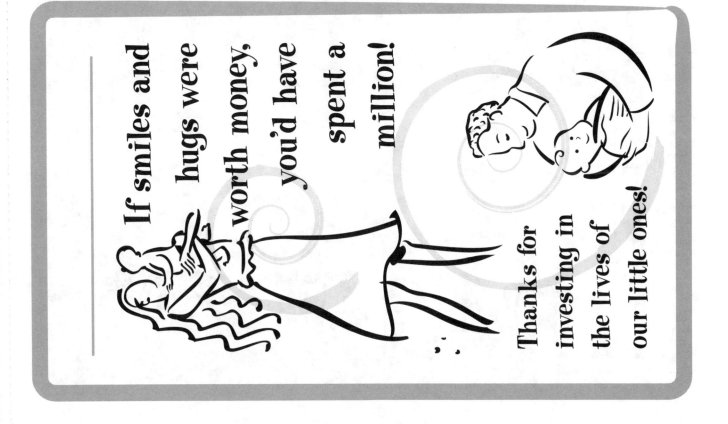

If **smiles** and **hugs** were **worth money,** **you'd have** **spent a** **million!**

Thanks for investing in the lives of our little ones!

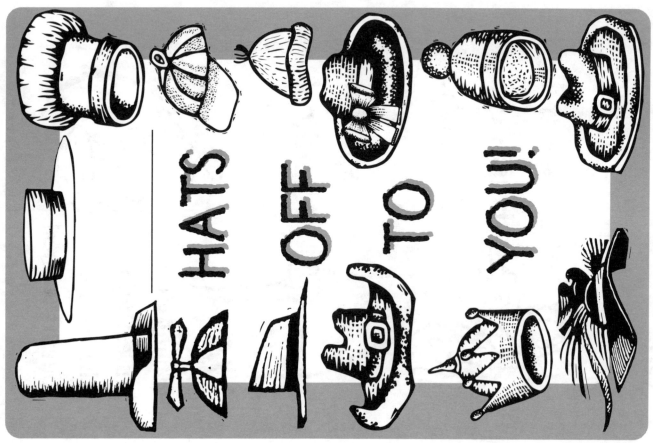

One, two, we thank you.

Three, four, we love you more.

Five, six and seven,
the reward's in heaven.

Eight, nine and ten,
come back again!

Favorite Friend Award

To _____

From _____

Wee Care Certificate
Awarded to

....

For

....

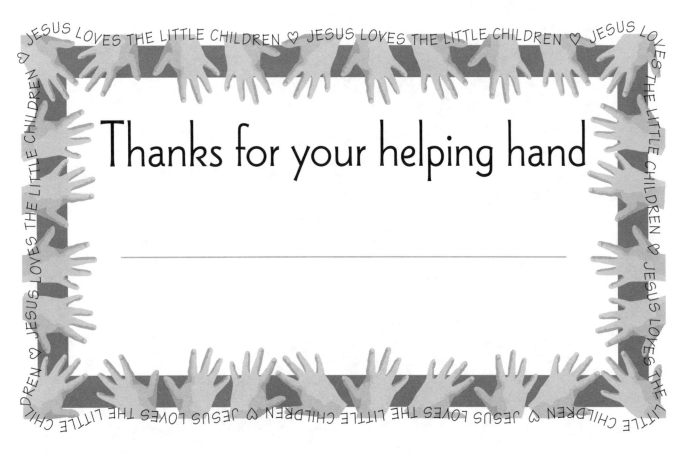

Thanks for your helping hand

_____

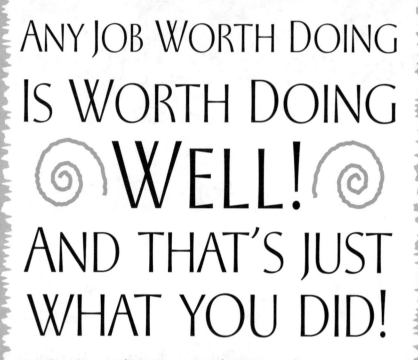

ANY JOB WORTH DOING
IS WORTH DOING
WELL!
AND THAT'S JUST
WHAT YOU DID!

THANKS,

As a Teacher You Are:

- [ ] a. Intelligent 
- [ ] b. Thoughtful 
- [ ] c. Loving 
- [ ] d. Creative 
- [x] e. All of the above

Thanks for everything!

Pizza Party

Thank you for your service in Children's Ministry!
We're serving you and your family

on _____

at _____

from _____ to _____ .

See you there!

Be
Our
Guest!

Teacher Appreciation BBQ

Date:

Time:

Place:

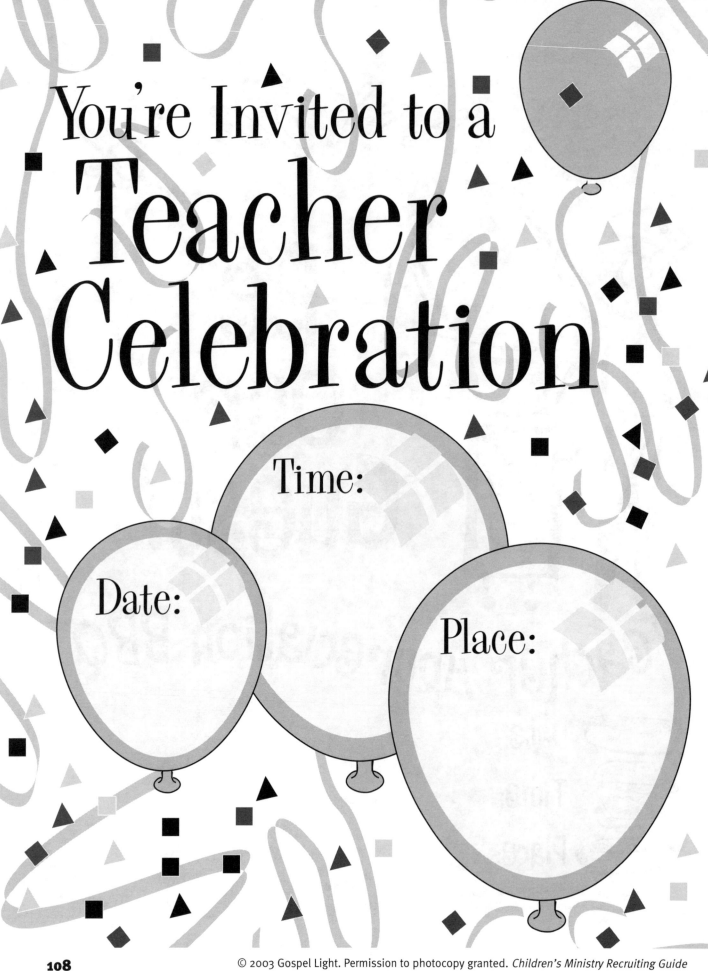

You're Invited to a
Teacher Celebration

Time:

Date:

Place:

Please Come to a

Thank-You Brunch

Date _____

Time _____

Place _____

R.S.V.P. _____

We're happy to honor YOU—

Who _____

_____

What _____

_____

When _____

Where _____

_____

Gracias

to all our volunteers!

You're invited to a
Children's Ministry Fiesta!

Date _____

Time _____

Place _____

A+ Teacher

All-Star Teacher

A Faithful Teacher

since

My teacher is a V.I.P.

Children's Ministry Volunteer

A Friend Like You

Ask several children to take turns reading the words of the song "A Friend Like You" 💿 as the narration for a montage of video clips or a slide show of photographs depicting children, staff and events from your children's ministry programs. Include a short invitation at the conclusion of the show.

1. I need a friend I can really depend on,

   Not just someone funny or cool—

   Someone who follows the Lord just like I do,

   Don't wanna be the friend of a fool.

   Friendship is a gift from God, a gift I can choose.

   I'm so glad He's brought me to you.

Chorus:

Oh, I thank God for a friend like you.

When I face a struggle, you help me through.

I know that your words will be wise and true,

So I thank God for sending me

A friend like you.

2. We always have fun when we're hangin' together;

   There's so much that we like to share.

   Trusting the Lord and respecting each other,

   I know we'll be honest and fair.

   We can always talk it out when we disagree,

   'Cause you love the Lord just like me.

Oh, I thank God for a friend like you.

When I face a struggle, you help me through.

I know that your words will be wise and true,

So I thank God for sending you.

Chorus

Words and Music by Jamie Owens Collins. © 2002 Fairhill Music, Inc. Used by permission.

Conclusion: The children in our church need you to be their friends. Opportunities for friendship building take place every Sunday morning. (Provide information about who to contact for further information about children's ministry.)

A Talk with Teachers

Videotape a number of the teachers and other workers from your children's ministry programs. Ask them two or three questions about children's ministry programs. Be sure to include people who work with a variety of different age levels. Choose from the following questions and/or write some of your own to fit the programs you offer:

- State your name and the age you teach.

- Why do you teach?

- How long have you been teaching?

- What's your favorite age to teach? Why?

- What are some words that describe kids in your class?

- What's the most important thing you do in children's ministry?

- What is something you do well in children's ministry? Something that excites you?

- What do you wish you could do better?

- What's the best moment you can remember in your class? The worst? The best teaching moment for you or your kids?

- What advice would you give to a new Sunday School teacher?

- Do you have any particular memories of your childhood Sunday School teachers?

- What would you say to someone who doesn't understand why you teach? Why do you give your time, commitment, etc.?

- What have you really enjoyed doing with kids in your class?

- What challenges do you face in teaching children?

- What challenges or needs do kids in your class face?

- Why do you think Sunday School is important for kids?

Introduce and conclude the video with the following narration:

Introduction: We'd like to introduce you to some of the stars of our children's ministry. Here is what they have to say about their experience in children's ministry.

Conclusion: While we can't measure the impact these teachers make in the lives of children, we know that God honors their commitment to sow the seed of His love. You can have a share in that harvest by becoming part of our children's ministry team. (Provide information about who to contact for information about children's ministry.)

Guess My Line!

This skit highlights some of the lesser known and underrated services performed by children's ministry workers. Use the people who actually do the jobs described, and tailor the script to fit the jobs performed at your church.

(At one side of the stage are three chairs for the panel. A podium is center stage. The three actors on the panel enter and take their seats. Host enters and stands at the podium.)

Emcee: Hello! And welcome to "Guess My Line!" I'm your Emcee, Terry Treehorn! *(Displays a big cheesy grin.)* Let's meet the judges! First, we have (Name each actor—when introduced, he or she stands, smiles and waves to the audience.)

Our guests are all members of our church who serve in children's ministries. Our panel of judges will get to ask questions to try and determine the UNUSUAL jobs of our guests. Let's meet our first guest!

Guest 1: *(Enters and stands next to Host at podium.)* Hi! I'm happy to be here. My name is (name).

Emcee: Let's get to the questions! Judge number 1?

Judge 1: Do you tell children Bible stories?

Guest 1: No.

Judge 2: Did you have to have special training to perform your job?

Guest 1: No.

Judge 3: Do you play a musical instrument?

Guest 1: No.

Emcee: Any guesses? *(Judges all look at each other and shrug their shoulders.)* Okay, it looks like you've stumped the panel with the questions. Now it's time to act out what your job entails!

(Guest 1 begins to pantomime punching out flannel figures for teachers to use as visual aids. Judges still appear to be stumped and ad-lib that they don't have any idea what Guest 1 is doing.)

Emcee: The judges still haven't got a clue. Does anyone in the audience? *(Whether or not anyone in the audience guesses correctly, the Host continues.)* Okay, (name of Guest 1) tell us your job!

Guest 1: I punch out flannel figures for teachers to use as visual aids when they tell their Bible stories. I work to help set supplies up for the teachers. *(Judges applaud.)*

Emcee: Thank you so much for coming on the show, and thank you for your valuable work for our kids! *(Guest 1 exits, smiling and waving as Guest 2 enters.)* I see our next guest is ready to go! Tell us your name, please.

Guest 2: (His or her name).

Emcee: Okay, judges, we're running out of time, so before you ask, we will tell you that this person does not tell Bible stories, did not need extensive training and does not play a musical instrument. In fact, it's a job that needs little more than a willingness to serve. (Name of Guest 2), please show us what you do.

(Guest 2 begins pantomiming counting out crackers and placing them on napkins, and/or pouring a drink into cups.)

Emcee: Okay, judges, surely you know what this person does!

Judges: *(In unison.)* Prepares snacks!

Guest 2: That's right!

Emcee: Thank you so much for coming on our show and for your service to the kids at our church. Well, folks, that's all for this edition of "Guess My Line!" *(Host and Judges exit.)*

Children's Leader: Punching out flannel figures or pouring cups of juice may not be the kinds of jobs people normally think of when they think about children's ministry workers. But every job is important. To the people who work directly with kids and the folks who help behind the scenes, we appreciate all that you do for our kids.

Sunday School Special

This skit is effective in introducing expressions of appreciation for those involved in the Sunday School, for thanking the congregation for supporting children's ministry, or for encouraging people to invite and bring neighborhood children to Sunday School. (This skit can be adapted for other children's programs.)

Jeremy: *(Shouting.)* Hey, Morgan! Come on out! I've got something to ask you!

Morgan: *(Offstage.)* Just a minute, Jeremy! I'm tying my shoes.

Jeremy: You'd better hurry, Morgan. This is important!

Morgan: *(Offstage.)* I'm coming! I'm coming! *(Enters.)* I'm here! So what's up?

Jeremy: I came over to ask if you can go to Sunday School with me tomorrow.

Morgan: Sunday School? I already go to school five days a week. Why would I want to go to school on Sunday?

Jeremy: Because it's a lot better than regular school. That's why we call it Sunday School. It's special!

Morgan: So why don't they call it Special School?

Jeremy: Because no one would know what day to come.

Morgan: Makes sense, I guess. But what do you do at Special School—I mean Sunday School?

Jeremy: What do we do? We do lots of stuff! Neat stuff!

Morgan: What kind of neat stuff?

Jeremy: *A*, we have art projects; *B*, we have Bible stories; *C*, we have contests; *D*, we have drama; *E*, we have—

Morgan: *(Interrupts.)* I'll bet you don't have anything for *Q* or *X* or *Z*.

Jeremy: *Q*, we have quizzes; *X*, we have excitement—

Morgan: *(Interrupts.)* That's cheating!

Jeremy: It was close enough. . . . and *Z*, we have a zillion other neat things!

Morgan:	Wow! A zillion! When is this Sunday School?
Jeremy:	On Sunday.
Morgan:	I knew that! I want to know what TIME on Sunday!
Jeremy:	It starts at 9:30! How about if we pick you up at 9:00 and we can be there a little early, 'cause our teachers always have some neat stuff ready, and we can get a head start on some of the other kids.
Morgan:	You're sure I'm gonna like it?
Jeremy:	Well, not totally sure. Remember, you're a little weird about things you like and don't like. *(Jeremy and Morgan begin to exit.)*
Morgan:	*(On the way out.)* What do you mean I'm weird? You're the one who eats apple-asparagus pie and won't try chocolate-covered cucumbers! *(They exit.)*
Children's Leader:	I think both Jeremy and Morgan may have a rather weird taste in snacks, but I'm sure that won't affect their enjoyment of our Sunday School. Every week a terrific team of teachers provides children with a marvelous hour of learning, packed with everything from *A* to *Z*—with possibly a few exceptions. On behalf of our children and their teachers, I want to express appreciation for the outstanding support you have given so that our children's ministry can continue to show God's love to the children of our church and our community.

T-E-A-C-H-E-R

This skit should be spoken as a cheer. All actors enter enthusiastically, smiling and lining up from stage right to stage left so that the word can be read by the audience as it is spelled out.

Actor 1: *(Enters, carrying a teacher manual and wearing around his or her neck a large sign with a T printed on it.) T is for the things you teach us.

Actor 2: *(Enters, carrying or juggling a few balls and/or beanbags and wearing around his or her neck a large sign with an E printed on it.) E is for exciting games.

Actor 3: *(Enters, carrying a large question mark drawn on a sheet of paper and wearing around his or her neck a large sign with an A printed on it.) A is for answers to our questions.

Actor 4: *(Enters, carrying a large paper heart and wearing around his or her neck a large sign with a C printed on it.) C is just because you care.

Actor 5: *(Enters, wearing around his or her neck a large sign with an H printed on it.) H is for the help you give us.

Actor 6: *(Enters, carrying a cookie and a paper cup and wearing around his or her neck a large sign with an E printed on it.) E is for the snacks we eat.

Actor 7: *(Enters, carrying an artist's pallet and wearing a beret and around his or her neck a large sign with an R printed on it.) R is for the art we do.

Actor 6: Hey! "Art" doesn't start with *R*! That's cheating!

Actor 7: *(Conspiratorially.) Shhh! Just go with it! (He or she smiles at the audience while* Actor 6 *shakes his or her head.)*

Actor 8: *(Enters, carrying a Bible and wearing around his or her neck a large sign with a B printed on it.) B is for the Bible that we study.

All: Put them all together they spell TEACHER . . . *(Pause.)* BUH.

(They exit together, jostling each other and ad-libbing about the extra letter at the end of the cheer: "How'd we end up with a B?" "BUH? What's that supposed to mean?" "Who wrote this thing, anyway?")

Children's Leader: We may have a little trouble spelling, but we don't have any trouble saying thank-you to the great teachers on our children's ministry staff. We're thankful to you and to God for the effort and love you give to the children in our church. Thank you!

© 2003 Gospel Light. Permission to photocopy granted. *Children's Ministry Recruiting Guide*

119

TEACHER FEATURE

All-Star Teachers

First Place Teachers

VIP

TEACHER

Teacher of the Month

Our Teachers Are Priceless!

 Like teacher, like child. Our teachers make a difference.

Thank you, Teachers!

Top reason our kids come to church? Teachers who care!

If you can find your way around in your Bible, thank a Sunday School teacher!

THUMBS-UP TO OUR TEACHERS!

SUNDAY SCHOOL TEACHERS AT WORK!
CHILDREN UNDER CONSTRUCTION

Our teachers share God's love from a child's perspective

Sunday after Sunday our teachers share their gifts

Loving hearts

Friendly faces

Caring hands

Listening ears

Our Sunday School—
Where Kids Meet Their Friends . . .
and Their **Best** Friend!

"Teaching kids to count is fine, but teaching them what counts is best."

Quality teaching brought to you from the Children's Ministry of our church

A message of God's love

in a big new world!

You Don't Run Across Durability Like This Every Day.

Since 1780 when the first Sunday School met, millions of people—children and adults—have learned how God's Word truly makes a difference in their lives.

FOUNDED 1780

LOVING CARE

BOTTLE

SAFETY

BABIES

TODDLERS

TOYS

NAPS

Our nursery is up to the challenge!

Here Are Some of the Many Little Reasons Our Church Has a Sunday School.

As you come to church each week, it doesn't take long to realize that our church is a family place. You'll see children smiling, laughing and talking as our church family gathers for a special time of learning about God's Word.

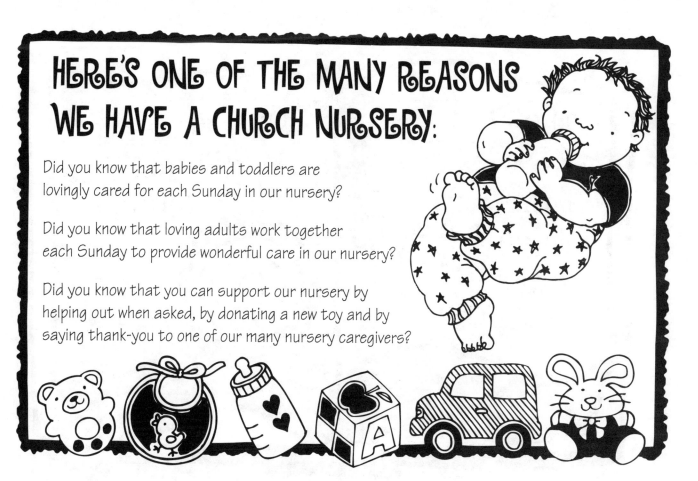

HERE'S ONE OF THE MANY REASONS WE HAVE A CHURCH NURSERY:

Did you know that babies and toddlers are lovingly cared for each Sunday in our nursery?

Did you know that loving adults work together each Sunday to provide wonderful care in our nursery?

Did you know that you can support our nursery by helping out when asked, by donating a new toy and by saying thank-you to one of our many nursery caregivers?

Overheard in the Nursery

"I MEET MORE VISITORS TO OUR CHURCH WHEN I WORK IN THE NURSERY THAN IN ANY OTHER PROGRAM I'VE EVER HELPED IN."
NURSERY CAREGIVER

"I HOPE THAT FRIENDLY LADY WITH THE BIG SMILE IS HERE TODAY."
ONE-YEAR-OLD

"THERE'S NO BETTER WAY TO GET A FRESH LOOK AT LIFE THAN TO WATCH A TODDLER EXPLORE."
NURSERY CAREGIVER

"I'VE BECOME A BETTER PARENT FROM WORKING IN THE NURSERY."
PARENT VOLUNTEER

"YOU FOUND MY FAVORITE BLANKET. YOU MUST LOVE ME!"
TWO-YEAR-OLD

There are no minor moments when you're teaching children.

Our teachers focus on what counts!

Our teachers come prepared!
- ✓ Bible stories to tell
- ✓ Games to play
- ✓ Songs to sing
- ✓ Bible verses to talk about
- ✓ Love for children

Children's Ministry

Sometimes it's hard to tell who's having the most fun!

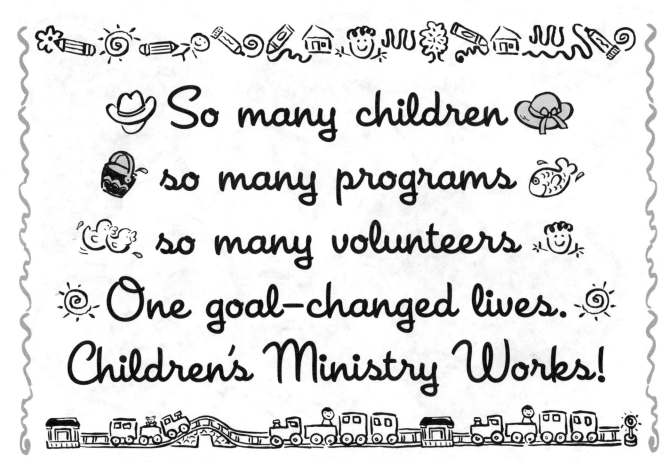

So many children
so many programs
so many volunteers
One goal—changed lives.
Children's Ministry Works!

using the CD-ROM

Contained on the *Children's Ministry Recruiting Guide* CD-ROM are three file formats:

1. **TIFF:** TIFF files are clip art images that **must be imported** into your word processing or page lay out application.

2. **PDF:** PDF files are awards, certificates, etc. They may be printed as is via Adobe® Acrobat® Reader®, or saved as EPS files and imported into most slide show, word processing and page layout applications.

3. **RTF:** RTF files are modifiable text files (no images). These files can be used by opening within your word processing or page layout application. Use these text files to create and print customized versions of files.

Please follow the instructions included for use of each file format.

TIFF Instructions

Important Notes: **You cannot open these files directly. These files may be too large for certain applications to be able to show you a preview.**

Here's what to do:

1. Open the application you wish to use.

2. Open an existing document or create a new document.

3. Paste (import) the TIFF into the document.

4. Enlarge or reduce the image according to your needs. (For specific instructions on how to use the image within your application, refer to your application manual.)

PDF Instructions

Important Notes: **PDF files can be opened and printed by anyone with the free Adobe Acrobat Reader software. PDF files on this CD-ROM cannot be modified via Adobe Acrobat Reader. We have included Acrobat Reader on the CD-ROM, or you can download the most recent version of Acrobat Reader for free from the Adobe website, http://www.adobe.com/products/acrobat/readstep.html.**

A PDF file cannot be inserted into most slide show or word applications. However, the PDF file can be saved as an EPS file following the few simple steps listed below in "Adapting PDF Files." The EPS file you create can be inserted as a picture file into most slide show and word applications.

Installation Instructions:

Follow the steps below to install a free copy of Adobe Acrobat Reader software from the *Children's Ministry Recruiting Guide* CD-ROM. If you already have Adobe Acrobat Reader on your computer, skip the following steps and proceed directly to "Here's what to do."

- Insert the CD-ROM into the CD-ROM drive.

- Open the Reader folder and then double-click on the Reader 5.0 Installer icon.

- Follow the on-screen directions to continue and click on the Install button if you agree to the terms. Once the installation is complete, restart your computer.

Here's what to do:

1. Double-click on the CD-ROM icon.

2. Double-click on the desired folder.

3. Double-click on the file you desire.

You may either print the files as is via Adobe Acrobat Reader, or adapt the files for use in a slide show or word application using instructions below.

Adapting PDF Files

Important Note: **The EPS file you create can be inserted as a picture file into most slide show and word applications.**

Here's what to do:

1. Open the PDF file using Adobe Acrobat Reader.

2. Go to the FILE menu on the toolbar. Select PAGE SETUP. Make sure page orientation matches the orientation of the image.

3. Go to the FILE menu on the toolbar. Select PRINT (this will bring up the PRINT dialog box).

    ▶ Change the Destination to FILE.
    ▶ Change General to SAVE AS FILE.
    ▶ Change Format to EPS STANDARD PREVIEW.

- ▶ Choose PostScript Level: LEVEL 2 AND 3.
- ▶ Choose Data Format: ASCII.
- ▶ No change needs to be made to Printer selection.

4. Select SAVE.

5. Save file to desired location.

Tips for using EPS files in Microsoft® PowerPoint® and Microsoft® Word

- When inserting an EPS file into Microsoft Word as a picture file, be sure to check the FLOAT OVER TEXT box when opening the EPS file. Please refer to your Microsoft Word manual for additional help.

- EPS files can not be directly edited in Microsoft PowerPoint or Microsoft Word. However, you can easily place a TEXT BOX over the image to personalize the document. Be sure to format the TEXT BOX with NO FILL and NO LINE. Please refer to your Microsoft Word manual for additional help.

- EPS files are generally larger than jpeg files, will use more memory and usually take longer to print.

- In order to edit the EPS file or save as a jpeg, you would need a page layout application such as Adobe® PhotoShop®, Adobe® Illustrator®, Quark™, etc.

RTF Instructions

Important Note: **You should not open these files directly. It is better to open the files from within the application you will use to edit the files.**

Rich Text Format (RTF) are modifiable text files. Most word applications, including Microsoft Word and WordPerfect, are able to read and edit RTF documents. Use these text files to create and print customized versions of documents.

Here's what to do:

1. Open the application you wish to use.

2. From within the application, open the file you wish to modify.

3. You can now edit the document.

4. Save the document in the standard document format of the application that you are using.

Problems?

If you have any problems that you can't solve by reading the manual that came with your word processing or page layout application, please call the number for the technical support department printed in your software manual. (Sorry, but Gospel Light cannot provide software support.)

Turn Good Volunteers into Great Teachers

Smart Teacher Training Videos are the smart, easy way to recruit, train and motivate teachers! Developed by Sunday School authorities Wes and Sheryl Haystead, each video includes expert advice, live classroom demonstrations and answers to the most common questions asked by teachers.

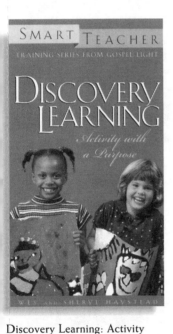

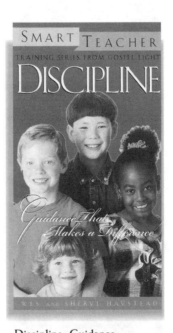

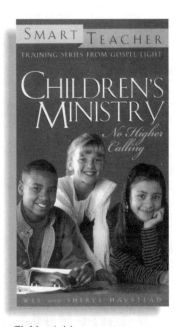

Discovery Learning: Activity with a Purpose

Guide children in the joy of discovering Bible truths for a lifetime of learning.
Video • UPC 607135.003601
$19.99

Bible Skills for Better Teaching: Helping Kids Make the Connection

How to connect Scripture to a child's experience, tell stories that come to life and share personal benefits of Bible study.
Video • UPC 607135.003588
$19.99

Discipline: Guidance That Makes a Difference

The loving way to prevent and correct disruptive behavior.
Video • UPC 607135.003618
$19.99

Children's Ministry: No Higher Calling

Challenge your teachers to consider the value Christ places on children and the astounding benefits ministry to children brings.
Video • UPC 607135.003595
$19.99

Available at your local Christian bookstore • www.gospellight.com

Gospel Light
God's Word for a Kid's World!™

Colorful Ways to Teach Kids About Jesus

God Answers Prayers
Shirley Dobson
Coloring Book
ISBN 08307.27507

God Loves You!
Shirley Dobson
Coloring Book
ISBN 08307.23293

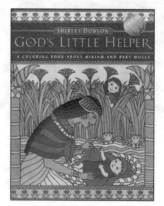

God's Little Helper
Shirley Dobson
Coloring Book
ISBN 08307.21886

God Made the World
Shirley Dobson
Coloring Book
ISBN 08307.24877

Growing as God's Child
Shirley Dobson
Coloring Book
ISBN 08307.26225

Jesus Is Alive!
Shirley Dobson
Coloring Book
UPC 607135.000891

Jesus Loves Me!
Shirley Dobson
Coloring Book
ISBN 08307.20715

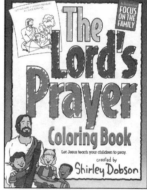

The Lord's Prayer
Shirley Dobson
Coloring Book
SPCN 25116.08987

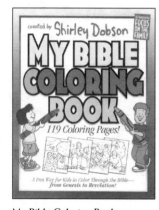

My Bible Coloring Book
Shirley Dobson
Coloring Book
ISBN 08307.20685

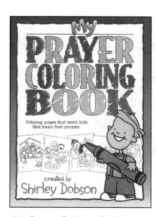

My Prayer Coloring Book
Shirley Dobson
Coloring Book
SPCN 25116.08251

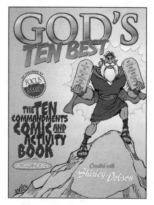

God's Ten Best:
The Ten Commandments
Comic and Activity Book
Shirley Dobson
Coloring Book
ISBN 08307.30605

God's Ten Best:
The Ten Commandments
Coloring Book
Shirley Dobson
Coloring Book
ISBN 08307.30613